# The Golden Cockerel

## The Art, Symbolism & History of the Stained Glass Windows St. Paul's Episcopal Church Key West, Florida

by
Winifred Shine Fryzel

Photography by
Scott Caldwell • Winifred Shine Fryzel • Monica Muñoz • Edwin O. Swift, III • Stephen Ehresman

Edited by
Barbara Hayo

Published by Historic Tours of America®
for St. Paul's Episcopal Church

www.historictours.com
www.stpaulskeywest.org
First Edition

Fryzel, Winifred Shine
     The Golden Cockerel. - 1st ed.


ISBN 978-0-9752698-5-5
ISBN 0-9752698-5-2


1.Stained Glass - History. 2. Churches - History. 3. Key West, FL - History. I. Title

# Dedication

*This work is dedicated to a Higher Authority*

# Hand of God

Holy Trinity or Te Deum – Window #125

# Contents

# Introduction and Acknowledgments

Key West lies in the path of dangerous hurricanes. Three former buildings of St. Paul's Episcopal Church have been destroyed, two by hurricane; one by fire. There is no assurance that the present and fourth church building can withstand the velocity of high winds and the strength of a tidal surge if the island is in the direct path of a major storm.

*The Golden Cockerel* is a documentary on the stained glass windows of this historic church. It serves not only as a detailed inventory of the windows, but also as a record of the past history of its congregation, residents of the island community. It accents the importance of focusing attention on preservation, and records a priceless heritage for future generations.

The work is not designed to be read from cover to cover. Each page is complete within itself, containing the story of the window and the documentary history of the window.

This book could not have been written alone. There were those who cheered its progress and those that gave the help needed for documentation. Dr. Herman K. Moore provided a computer which made the work easier. Tom Hambright of the Florida Division of the Monroe County Library gave untiringly of his time and expertise. Bob Jones, member of the Stained Glass Association of America, kept in touch with valuable information that could not have been obtained without him. When the church building was being repaired, photographer Scott Caldwell climbed the scaffolding and provided detailed photographs of outstanding beauty. – ***Winifred Shine Fryzel***

# Foreword

For Ed Swift, President of Historic Tours of America®, the decision to publish *The Golden Cockerel* came from his deep appreciation for Winifred Shine Fryzel and her special generation of local residents whose memories of the island reach way beyond his, and from his personal passion for the preservation of the history of Key West. When he asked me to edit this remarkable book, I was honored.

One afternoon, as I sat in the quiet coolness of St. Paul's Church, manuscript in hand, surrounded by the glorious medium of color and light, watching a few tourists walk through in respectful silence and wondering where to start, a very personal connectivity came to light.

Sitting there, just steps beyond the hubbub of Duval Street, I felt surrounded by a transcendental aura I experience any time I am in an "old world" church where I am innately comfortable with the familiar. As a child I visited numerous European Gothic cathedrals and recall being awed by the towering coldness, yet warmed by the incredible colored light streaming through the enormous glass walls. I used to imagine what it must have been like in 12th and 13th centuries, when life was so hard and grim, to enter a church and in its overwhelming vastness feel the presence of God.

As I looked closely at the windows in St. Paul's, I came to appreciate them as Winifred Fryzel intended: as works of ecclesiastic art and as a documentation of the history of the people of Key West, from pioneer to present. *The Golden Cockerel* is as much a story of the people of Key West as it is of the Old Testament prophecy and New Testament stories told through its lovely windows.

Studying the windows, stories from the Bible, learned in my own Anglican upbringing, came back to me. Reading the names on the memorials on each window, familiar Key West names such as Porter, Lowe, Curry, Bartlum and Bethel brought to mind the island's history of sea captains, wreckers, cigar makers, lighthouse keepers, spongers, doctors and merchants, whose roots were in New England and the Bahamas.

Matching window to manuscript, I learned of some less familiar parishioners such as the Shacklefords, a black family with roots in pre-civil war Missouri, who came to Key West sometime prior to 1874. In windows donated by the Flower Guild, whose flowers for the altar came from the ladies' own gardens, I thought of the warm bonds formed by work in the church for a collective purpose. In the Baptistry, I was moved by the windows poignantly dedicated to young lives lost. Taken together as a body of work the windows, as memorials, serve as a reminder that the church was the social, as well as spiritual center of the parishioners' lives, and very often held the only records of their genealogy. St. Paul's Episcopal Church was, and still is, a diverse family, welcoming the wealthy, the humble, the distinguished and the anonymous.

In our mission of placing Winifred Fryzel's impeccable research on the windows as art and as memorials within the context of the church as a whole, we have taken the liberty to elaborate on some of the text. We have included a brief history of St. Paul's Church; added to the story of stained glass; expanded on the symbolism of the title; supplied additional information on the history of Key West; and, where appropriate, included edification of the symbolism.

In order to enhance the use of the book as a companion piece to viewing the windows, we have changed the window number sequence from the original manuscript. The story of the windows begins with those on the lower level of the Baptistry and moves in numeric sequence around the church in a counterclockwise direction. Once back at the Baptistry, the sequence resumes on the upper level.

Our thanks are extended to David Eyer for his informative tour of the church and input, and to The Reverend David Wilt, for his gracious support of our role in this endeavor.

As an Episcopal church in an island setting, with a history dating back to its first settlers, St. Paul's has a special quality. While the church's traditional Anglican rituals are deeply rooted, just as the stained glass windows down the length of the nave were designed to open to the tropical breeze, its doors are open to all who choose to enter. St. Paul's reflects and is deeply connected to the island community it serves.

Winifred Fryzel's labor of love allows us to experience each window on three levels: the aesthetic, the spiritual and the historic. If all those who enter the church can leave with a sense of all three, our collective objective will have been accomplished. – *Barbara Hayo*

High Altar of St. Paul's

View from the High Altar

# Preface

When I was called to St. Paul's Episcopal Church as rector in March of 2004, I had already seen the magnificent stained glass windows from previous visits to Key West. Little did I know the spiritual impact these windows have until I was able to see them on a daily basis. The facets, the colors, certainly every aspect of each window are continuously telling a Biblical story.

Additionally, these windows tell, over and over again, the love that people have for one another and for cherished family by these gifts that have been offered to the glory of God over the many decades.

I am also amazed at the awe and respect these wonderful windows demand. Often as I walk through the sanctuary during the day, I find people sitting quietly, or walking slowly around the perimeter, entranced by the beauty before them. Not a day goes by when someone in a hushed voice asks if they are permitted to take pictures of the windows. I always assure them that they are welcome to do so, that these windows are there for their spiritual uplifting and joy, and offer not the glory of St. Paul's, but the glory of God.

Finally, I was not in Key West very long before I was introduced to an amazing woman. Winifred Shine Fryzel has spent a lifetime archiving the many historic items and events that have been so much of St. Paul's heritage and legacy. Her effort to put together the history of the St. Paul's windows is a living testament to her love for her church. To be privileged to sit and talk with Winifred about the history of St. Paul's is truly a joy in my life.

God has been good to St. Paul's in her 173 years of existence by bringing her many faithful and generous servants. It is my hope and prayer that those who read this account of St. Paul's and her glorious windows will be inspired to continue in the support of this historic place or be compelled to look at your own place of worship with a renewed sense of what the term "holy space' means.

Faithfully,

**The Rev. David R. Wilt**
32nd Rector
St. Paul's Episcopal Church
Key West, Florida

May 2005

by George Carey

# St. Paul's Episcopal Church

# St. Paul's Episcopal Church
## Key West, Florida

*In Key West: The Old and the New (1912),* Jefferson Browne describes the earliest days of the settlement of Key West in the early1820s as a sparsely populated, barren, isolated place with no more than 10 families. There were no churches and, as the population grew, people gathered in various locations for non-denominational services. Occasionally a clergyman would pass through and his services would be engaged, with no concern of his denomination.

On March 7, 1831, the first movement was made to have a permanent clergyman come to Key West. According to Browne, the Episcopal Church was the pioneer religious organization in Key West, and the entire population who desired a church to be established for the purpose of public devotion did so under the

*Second Church 1848-1886. The photo dates from 1875. This church was destroyed during the great fire of 1886.*

name of the Protestant Episcopal Church. The Reverend Sanson K. Brunot, only 24 years old and very new to the ministry, was welcomed to the island on December 23, 1832. Two days later, on Christmas Day, the first service of the Episcopal Church by a regularly ordained minister was held in Key West. As there was no church building in which to hold the service, it was held in Jackson Square, in the first court house.

On that same day, the first Episcopal congregation was formed. On February 4, 1833, the parish organized and a charter was obtained for St. Paul's Church, Key West, making it the oldest church parish in all of Florida south of St. Augustine. On May 5, 1838, Mrs. John William Charles Fleming gave the vestry of St. Paul's Church the land of its present location, on the corner of Duval and Eaton Streets. Mrs. Fleming was the widow of John W. C. Fleming who, in 1822 purchased 1/4 of the island of Key West from John W. Simonton, who had purchased it some months earlier on December 20, 1821 from its original owner, Juan Pablo Salas of St. Augustine.

Mrs. Fleming's land donation came with two provisos: the pews were to be forever free (it was customary in those days for families to purchase family pews, reserved only for their use), and her husband, who passed away on December 18, 1832, one week before the first service, would be buried in the church grounds. To this date her wishes have been honored.

The pews are open to all and it is presumed that Mr. Fleming is buried under the chancel of the present church which had been built over the cemetery garden of the previous church. In addition to Mr. Fleming, five others remain buried under the present church: Miss Hallet, Fielding A. Browne, Lt. B.C. Edes, Angela Silvania and Alexander Denham. All other buried there were moved to the Key West Cemetery. A marble slab memorializing Mr. Fleming is set into the wall of the north transept.

Throughout its history, a series of catastrophic events caused St. Paul's congregation to have to build three churches on the same site before the present church was completed in 1919. According to Browne, the first church, made of coral rock, was nearly completed in May 1846, eight years after the land donation, but was blown down by a hurricane on October 11th of that same year. A new frame church built on the site was ready for the first service two years later, on July 30, 1848. This second church was destroyed in the great fire of 1886, which destroyed much of the commercial area of Key West. Yet another frame church was built on the site until it, too, was destroyed, this time by a hurricane on October 11, 1909, ironically on the same day and month as the hurricane that destroyed the first church.

Concrete was chosen for the fourth and present church on which construction began in 1914. The building was constructed on the same land, but on a different site than the previous three. The entrance to the earlier churches had been on Eaton Street. Much to the chagrin of many parishioners comfortable with the way things were, the vestry approved a design by architect George Pfeiffer to situate the church in the traditional manner, with the altar in the east end of the cruciform church, thereby placing the portals on Duval Street.

*Third Church 1888-1909.*
*The photo dates from 1895 and shows the Church and Rectory as seen from Eaton Street.*
*The inset shows The Reverend Gilbert Higgs, Rector of St. Paul's.*
*The third church was destroyed during a hurricane in 1909.*

# The Architect

## GEORGE L. PFEIFFER

Following the complete destruction of the third church in the hurricane of October 11, 1909, St. Paul's building committee proposed that the next church be constructed of concrete. This choice of materials was undoubtedly influenced by the building of Henry Flagler's Key West Extension of the Florida East Coast Railway in progress at the time. The strength of reinforced concrete used on the numerous railroad bridges and viaducts that spanned the length of the Florida Keys, a phenomenal feat at the time, most assuredly had impressed many residents.

The proposal to build the church structure of concrete was accepted at the annual meeting held on Easter Monday 1911. Well-known Miami architect, George L. Pfeiffer, was engaged to work for 2 1/2% of the cost of the building.

According to Miami historian Thelma Peters, author of *Lemon City*, a history of early Miami, George L. Pfeiffer was born in 1861 in Germany. He came to the United States in 1893 to see the World's Fair and a few years later moved to Miami where he purchased a home in a pioneer community on the shores of Biscayne Bay known as Lemon City.

Pfeiffer's Miami architecture reflected his belief that buildings should be oriented to catch the prevailing breezes through cross ventilations, high ceilings and shaded porches. He brought this philosophy to the design of St. Paul's. It is believed that given the size and position of the lot, Mr. Pfeiffer did his best to design the church to take advantage of the prevailing southeast cooling winds of the spring and summer. This is evident in the lower level stained glass windows which pivot to catch the faintest breeze, in the high ceilings, and in the shaded cloister. For a time, even the two windows featuring Saint Paul, which flank the *Crucifixion* to form the grand east wall window over the High Altar, opened with a pulley system to let in the breeze.

Pfeiffer also proposed that the rectory be removed from its location on the corner of Eaton and Duval Streets in order to erect the new church in that location, with its west portals opening onto Duval Street. By April of 1914, the rectory was moved to its present site and construction on the new church began. On Whitsunday, June 8, 1919, the first service was held in the new church.

# The Glass Studios

The 12th and 13th centuries in Europe were termed the "Golden Age of Glass," as the Gothic age produced the great cathedrals of Europe and brought a full flowering of stained glass windows. Medieval churches with their translucent pictures of biblical stories and saints' lives made them a sacred dwelling place of an all powerful God.

The Renaissance, however, with its focus on painters, brought the art of stained glass into a 300 year period where windows were heavily painted white glass, with lead lines becoming decorative elements only. As a result of this painterly trend, during the 18th century many of the medieval stained glass windows were removed and replaced by painted glass. Thus the art of colored glass faceted with lead all but died until the late 1800s when glass studios in England once again became prominent.

The Bolton Brothers, English immigrants, established the first stained glass studios in America. At the turn of the 20th century, the revival of the traditional art of stained glass swept America and new designs and techniques were introduced by American glass artists such as Louis Comfort Tiffany, George Hardy Payne, Richard Spiers, Wilbur Burnham, and others.

The stained glass windows in St. Paul's Episcopal Church in Key West represent over 80 years of American stained glass. The remoteness the island did not for a moment deter the parishioners of St. Paul's from commissioning some of America's most recognized stained glass studios for the work in their church. Well-known national firms such as Phipps, Ball & Burnham, Payne Spiers and Charles Connick Associates, whose works grace such major churches as the National Cathedral in Washington and the Cathedral of St. John the Divine in New York City, were contracted to bring their work to Key West.

That these island parishioners were aware of the stained glass movement in the United States and chose the very best in the nation for the glass work in their church, is a tribute to their worldliness. Although in a remote location, the islanders were by no means isolated and unsophisticated. Sailing ships from all over the world passed through the strategic port of Key West, long known as the "Gibraltar of the Caribbean." Many Key West residents were involved in some aspect of the lucrative shipping trade and traveled all over the world, acquiring fine artistic tastes from the far reaches of the globe. Some passengers and crew aboard the many sailing vessels traveling the shipping lanes of the Gulf Stream, who stopped at the busy seaport of Key West, decided to stay, bringing with them ideas and tastes from their former homes. Yet another source of global influence on Key West was its strong business and familial ties with Havana, an elegant old world Spanish city.

Today the doors of St. Paul's Church are open daily for all those who wish to enter for prayer and meditation, or simply to experience its beauty. Unfortunately for passersby, the beauty of the stained glass windows cannot be appreciated from the outside as they are protected from damage by a strong, translucent plastic material placed over the window exterior. While offering some degree of protection from wind-driven objects and hurricane force winds, this covering has yellowed with age, effectively obscuring the images from the outside. There is currently an effort underway to secure funds to protect these priceless windows with new hurricane-rated clear glass. This improvement would not only provide optimum protection, but would also allow the glorious windows to be appreciated both inside and out.

**Stained Glass Studios represented in the windows of St. Paul's Church**
**Phipps, Ball & Burnham (1920)**
**Payne Spiers Studio (1940)**
**Charles Connick Associates (1950)**
**Harry Taylor (1970)**
**Powell Brothers & Sons Glass Art (1999-2005)**

# PHIPPS, BALL & BURNHAM

Over one-half of the stained glass windows in St. Paul's Church were designed and installed by Phipps, Ball & Burnham in the 1920s, immediately following the construction of the church.

The studio is responsible for all windows featuring roundels, circular themed panels, each depicting a different "Sign of Our Faith." These windows are long and rectangular, centered by an embellished cross with a roundel placed where the arms intersect, set against a background of opalescent glass. Each roundel contains a different religious symbol. A series of roundel windows along the lower level of the nave and in the north and south transept, open for ventilation. Roundels are also featured in the stationary south tower and bell tower clerestory windows.

Phipps, Ball and Burnham is also responsible for the major narrative windows positioned in the four compass corners of the cruciform church. On the east end, in the chancel over the High Altar is *Crucifixion* (Window #117) *Nativity Adoration* (Window #112) is in the south transept clerestory; *Ascension/Pentecost/Resurrection* (Window #122) is on the opposing wall, in the north transept clerestory; and Christ's genealogy, depicted in *Jesse Tree* (Window #102) is in the clerestory over the Baptistry at the west end of the church.

Two narrower Phipps, Ball & Burnham windows, appropriately occupying a place of honor on either side of *Crucifixion* over the high altar, feature St. Paul, for whom the church is named. The choice of the Apostle Paul as the patron saint of the church undoubtedly came from the connectivity between one of the stories of Paul the Evangelist and the history of Key West. As told in *Acts 27,28*, Saint Paul survived both a hurricane lasting fourteen days and a subsequent shipwreck.

When these first windows were initially commissioned, Phipps, Ball & Burnham was called Ball & Burnham. In the vestry minutes of St. Paul's it is recorded that Mr. Ball was in Key West on July 14, 1919, and having already in hand a number of contracts for these memorials, he submitted a proposition to furnish cathedral glass windows for the lower openings and tower for about $1300.00. At that meeting the vestry signed an agreement for placing the Sunday School window in the chancel. According to St. Paul's history, the actual window installation began in 1920. By this time the firm's name had changed to Phipps, Ball & Burnham; by 1922 it was in the name of Burnham alone.

Wilbur Herbert Burnham was born in Boston on February 4, 1887, the son of Wilbur Leroy and Mary (Oxley) Burnham. He was educated at East Boston High School and studied at Massachusetts School of Art from 1904-08. He also studied stained glass in France, England, Italy and Spain.

He began his career as a designer of stained glass for Harry Goodhue in Boston, working there from 1906-1916. He worked for Horace J. Phipps Company of Boston from 1916-18; from 1918-1920, he was in business with Ball and Burnham. The firm then became Phipps, Ball and Burnham until it was dissolved in 1922, leaving only Burnham at the helm.

Burnham, along with Charles J. Connick and Joseph G. Reynolds, comprised a triumvirate of nationally prominent glass designers in Boston. Some of Burnham's stained glass efforts are represented in the Cathedral of St. John the Divine (10 windows), the Washington National Cathedral, Riverside Church in New York City, and Rollins College in Winter Park, Florida.

Wilbur Herbert Burnham, artist and designer of stained glass windows, died at Melrose-Wakefield Hospital in his 87th year.

Of Burnham's thirty-seven windows in St. Paul's Church, Bob Jones of the Stained Glass Association of America noted in a letter dated July 13, 1995: "Burnham was held in such esteem, and this is *a*, if not *the*, most important assemblage of his early work."

# PAYNE SPIERS

Richard Spiers was one of the leading stained glass artists of the American revival of the traditional art of stained glass during the early 20th century, while George Payne was a well-known glass maker whose business dated back to 1875. Spiers' son, George, joined forces in 1935 with George Leslie Payne, grandson of the George Payne, to create Payne Spiers, located in Patterson, New Jersey. The two worked together from 1935 until 1946, and were responsible for numerous magnificent stained glass windows in many churches throughout America in the 1940s.

In St. Paul's Church, the Payne Spiers studio created *Wedding Feast at Cana* (Window #109) and *Feeding of the Five-Thousand* (Window #107), both in the south nave clerestory. These magnificent narrative windows depict two of the miracles of Jesus.

Payne Spiers is also responsible for the incredibly beautiful and intricate wood reredos behind the High Altar, donated by George and Julia Johnson, Hiram and Leonora Seymour, Lillian Louisa Bartlum, Nellie Isabelle Curry, and John and Eliza Pitcher.

# CHARLES J. CONNICK ASSOCIATES

Four windows in St. Paul's Church were designed by Charles J. Connick Associates, another major American glass studio: *Christ Among the Doctors* (Window #108) in the south nave clerestory; *Transfiguration* (Window #127) in the north nave clerestory; and the two prophesy windows, *Genealogy Window – Prophets* (Window #101 and 103), flanking Phipps, Ball & Burnham's *Jesse Tree* to create the great west window in the clerestory above the Baptistery.

Although Charles J. Connick died in 1945, before the windows were installed, the studio continued under the direction of the very able Orin E. Skinner. In an article in the *Quarterly of the Stained Glass Association of America* (Volume 88, Number 2, Summer 1993), from 1920 until his death Charles Connick counted on his "left-handed, right hand man," Orin Skinner, to get the job done. Connick was the spark plug of the studio and liberally delegated the daily responsibilities to his assistants. Orin Skinner handled the art, production, scheduling, personnel, sales and installation. Elizabeth Bruder ran the front office, scheduled appointments, kept the books and paid the bills. With this system, Charles J. Connick became the most influential and successful proponent of stained glass in America and was considered the leading American expert in his day in the stained glass field.

With the death of Connick, the studio continued to operate under his name. With Skinner as president and Mrs. Bruder in the front office, the studio maintained the high quality for which it was known. Skinner said that when Connick died, he had an awful time trying to convince people that the business would continue. He succeeded, and the studio continued for 41 years under his direction with no shortcuts to the perfection or craftsmanship.

From the opening of the studio in Boston in 1913 until it closed in 1986, the artists in the Connick studio led the American revival of the medieval style of the stained glass craft through their use of intense color and strong linear design. Windows created by the Connick studio can be found in approximately 5,000 churches and public buildings around the world. When the studio closed, it gave its collection of records and working drawings to the Boston Public Library.

# HARRY TAYLOR

Harry Taylor is the only local stained glass artist whose work is represented in St. Paul's. Little is known about Harry Taylor except for an article that appeared in the *Miami Herald* on July 14, 1968. The article states that Harry was from the Midwest, was 75 years old and was employed at Speas Glass Company in Key West.

Although Taylor worked in the field of ornamental glass all his life, he did not practice it in Key West until 1963. He was contacted by the church in 1968 to repair *Nativity Adoration* (Window #112). At a later date, at age 84, he was commissioned to create *Christ with the Elders* (Window #110) in the south transept and *Christ with the Fishermen* (Window #124) in the north transept.

# POWELL BROTHERS & SONS GLASS ART

Powell Brothers & Sons Glass Art is a family business in Salt Lake City, Utah which has been creating works of glass art for more than 30 years. Specializing in traditional stained and painted glass, they create artworks for settings around the world. Trained in glasswork by American and European instructors, the Powells have designed many works to be integrated into existing structures.

The lead Powell Brothers artists of their four chancel windows: *Zacchaeus Climbing the Sycamore Tree* (Window #119); *Deborah and a Scroll Under the Palms* (Window #115); *Saint Barnabas* (Window #114); and *Miriam* (Window #120) were Jenkyn A. Powell and his son, J. Elijah Powell. Powell Brothers also designed and installed the four windows inside the choir room and two in the sacristy. The latter windows are not visible from the sanctuary.

The Powell Studio is recognized as one of America's leading glass studios and has affiliations with the International Guild of Glass Artists. It is a member of the AIA Interfaith Forum on Religion, Art and Architecture, and is an Accredited Full Service Studio Member of the Stained Glass Association of America.

# UNKNOWN STUDIOS

For 10 windows there has been no record found to date of the artist, the studio or the installer. Therefore no credit can be given. It is possible that *Holy Trinity/Te Deum* (Window #125), attributable to Phipps, Ball & Burnham, was made by F.X. Zetler of Munich. However, there is no documentation to confirm that speculation.

# Window Layout – Lower Level

|  | Sacristy |  | High Altar |  | Choir<br>Room |  |
|---|---|---|---|---|---|---|

| | | | |
|---|---|---|---|
| 19 | **North** | | **South** 18 |
| 20 | **Transept** | | **Transept** 17 |
| 21 | | | 16 |
| 22 | | | 15 |
| 23 | | | 14 |

*Eaton Street*

| | | |
|---|---|---|
| 24 | | 13 |
| 25 | | 12 |
| 26 | | 11 |
| 27 | **Nave** | 10 |
| 28 | | 9 |
| 29 | | 8 |

**Bell<br>Tower**                                           **South<br>Tower**

**Baptistry**

**North<br>Portal**       1-2       3-4-5       6-7

*Duval Street*

| | | |
|---|---|---|
| #1 Flight Into Egypt | #11 Mitre Roundel | #21 Saint Matthew Roundel |
| #2 Guardian Angel | #12 Holy Spirit Roundel | #22 IHS Roundel |
| #3 Baptism of Jesus | #13 Agnus Dei Roundel | #23 Christ w/Woman of Samaria |
| #4 Jesus Blessing Little Children | #14 Presentation of Jesus | #24 Cross & Crown Roundel |
| #5 Phillip and the Ethiopian | #15 Chi Rho Roundel | #25 Chalice and Cruets Roundel |
| #6 Guardian Angel | #16 Chalice Roundel | #26 Saint Luke Roundel |
| #7 Moses Smiting the Rock | #17 Alpha and Omega Roundel | #27 Font Roundel |
| #8 Holy Trinity Roundel | #18 Annunciation of Our Lady | #28 Saint Mark Roundel |
| #9 Saint John Roundel | #19 Raising Jairus' Daughter | #29 Cross and Anchor Roundel |
| #10 Pomegranate Roundel | #20 Chi Rho Roundel | |

**Glass Studio Legend:**

| | |
|---|---|
| *Phipps, Ball & Burnham (1920)* | RED |
| *Payne Spiers (1940)* | PINK |
| *Charles Connick Associates (1950)* | GREEN |
| *Harry Taylor (1970)* | PURPLE |
| *Powell Brothers (1999-2003)* | AQUA |
| *Unknown* | BLUE |

# Window Layout – Upper Level

```
                        118        117       116
            Sacristy    119    High Altar    115      Choir
                        120                  114      Room


        121                                        113
           North                                      South
        122 Transept                          Transept 112


        123                                        111
           124                                    110



                         125              109
    Eaton Street




                         126              108
                             Nave



                         127              107



                  128                 106
            Bell  129                 105     South
            Tower 130                 104     Tower


                          Baptistry
                North
                Portal   101    102    103
                          Duval St.
```

## Upper Level Windows

| | | |
|---|---|---|
| #101 Genealogy (Prophets) | #111 Saint Luke | #121 Saint Mark |
| #102 Jesse Tree Window | #112 Nativity Adoration | #122 Resurrection |
| #103 Genealogy (Prophets) | #113 Saint John | #123 Saint Matthew |
| #104 INRI Roundel | #114 Saint Barnabas | #124 Christ with Fishermen |
| #105 Cock Roundel | #115 Deborah & Scrolls | #125 Holy Trinity |
| #106 Sword of the Spirit Roundel | #116 St Paul on Mars Hill | #126 Entry Into Jerusalem |
| #107 Feeding the Five Thousand | #117 Crucifixion | #127 Transfiguration |
| #108 Christ Among the Doctors | #118 Saint Paul on Road to Damascus | #128 Cross & Keys Roundel |
| #109 Wedding Feast at Cana | #119 Zacchaeus Climbing Tree | #129 St. Andrew Roundel |
| #110 Christ with the Elders | #120 Miriam | #130 Pillar & Scourge Rounde |

## Glass Studio Legend:

| | |
|---|---|
| *Phipps, Ball & Burnham (1920)* | **RED** |
| *Payne Spiers (1940)* | PINK |
| *Charles Connick Associates (1950)* | **GREEN** |
| *Harry Taylor (1970)* | **PURPLE** |
| *Powell Brothers (1999-2003)* | **AQUA** |
| *Unknown* | **BLUE** |

# The Symbolism of the Golden Cockerel

The title of the book is inspired by the image of the cock in one of the stained glass windows in the church, *Cock Roundel* (Window #105) by Phipps, Ball & Burnham, installed under the initial contract in 1920. The cock in the roundel stands vigil over the nave from its perch in the center panel of the south tower window. Upon entering the church through the north portal, *Cock Roundel* is easily visible by looking up and straight ahead before turning to the left to look at the altar, as one might be inclined to do.

In Christian symbolism, the cock, or rooster, has several meanings. One is as a symbol of the Apostle Peter. The symbolism relates to the cock crowing during the Passion, the incident that caused Peter to realize his betrayal of Christ.

During the Last Supper, Christ told Peter that Peter would deny Him three times before the cock crowed. Peter denied that he would ever forsake His Lord, yet out of fear, he did. After Jesus was arrested, Peter, careful to stay at safe distance, went along to the official buildings to see what was to transpire. While there, Peter was recognized and, as predicted by Jesus earlier, denied Him three times. At dawn, when Peter heard the cock crow, he remembered the words of Jesus and wept. The symbol of the cock therefore stands as a reminder to all to not give in to our human fear, but to remain faithful to Christ. The cock on the spires of many churches also is said to call all men to repent as Peter repented.

Another interpretation of the cock as a Christian symbol is one of vigilance and protection. By interpretive extrapolation, Peter, whose symbol is the cock, is called Peter, the rock, by Jesus. In Hebrew, rock has many meanings, one of those is God's protection.

Of special significance to St. Paul's Church, for over 63 years few knew the cock kept watch in the south tower as little natural light came through the window. In the spring of 1994, the window was illuminated by artificial means, lighting up the nave, bringing completeness to the church.

# Dedication of Stained Glass Windows

We present to you these Stained Glass Windows to be set apart for the service of Christ's holy Church.

Priest: All things come from you, O Lord;

People: *And from your own gifts do we give to you.*

Priest: Prosper the work of our hands;

People: *Prosper our handiwork.*

Priest: Show your servants your works;

People: *And your splendor to their children.*

Let us pray.

Almighty God, we thank you that you have put it into the hearts of your people to make offerings for your service, and have been please to accept their gifts. Be with us now and bless us as we set apart these windows to your praise and glory and in memory and honor of (*name*), through Jesus Christ our Lord. *Amen*

*Antiphon*

I will make your windows of agates, and all your borders of pleasant stones.

Priest: Look upon the rainbow, and praise him who made it;

People: *How beautiful it is in its brightness.*

Let us pray. (*Silence*)

O Lord God, the whole world is filled with the radiance of your glory: Accept our offering of these windows which we now dedicate to you for adornment of this place and the inspiration of your people. Grant that as the light shines through them in many colors, so our lives may show forth the beauty of your manifold gifts of grace; through Jesus Christ our Lord. *Amen*

Almighty God, we remember you today your faithful servants, (*name*), and we pray that, having opened to them the gates of larger life, you will receive them more and more into your joyful service, that, with all who have faithfully served you in the past, they may share in the eternal victory of Jesus Christ our Lord.

*Amen*

**13**

# Window #1
# Flight into Egypt

**Phipps, Ball & Burnham (Conjecture)**
**1920 (before 1950)**
**64" x 26 3/4"**

*In Loving Memory of*
*Capt. George H. Bocker    Apr. 17, 1834 – Sept. 17, 1915 &*
*Gertrude L. Bocker    Apr. 20, 1854 – Dec. 18, 1918*

**DESCRIPTION:** In this narrative stained glass window, Mary is seated on a donkey holding the Child, while Joseph leads the animal. The detail shows the Holy Mother dressed in white with a long blue cloak about her shoulders. Her headdress is draped in loose folds about her figure. She is holding the peacefully sleeping Child who is portrayed in a realistic manner.

**SYMBOLISM:** The nimbus surrounding Mary's head distinguishes her as a saint. The origin is of great antiquity. Rays of light or fire were ancient emblems of divine power. The Tri-Radiant surrounding the head of the Child is used entirely for the representation of the Father, Son and Holy Ghost.

**MEMORIAL:** Although the parents of George H. Bocker were from Germany, he was born in Belgium. He entered the United States at the age of 14 and became a naturalized citizen in 1872, the same year that he married Gertrude S. Davis. Their marriage on June 22, 1872, was performed by The Reverend Charles A. Fulwood at the Old Stone Methodist Church.

Gertrude was born in Florida. Her father was born in Ireland; her mother in the Bahamas. Gertrude and George were parents of a son born in 1878 and a daughter, Rosalie, born in 1884. The 1900 census lists George H. Bocker as a sea captain, a historically important profession in Key West at the time. The family resided at 526 Angela Street.

Flight into Egypt

# Window #2
# Guardian Angel

**Studio Unknown**
**Circa 1975**
**61 1/2" x 20 1/2"**

**DESCRIPTION:** The modern window is one of a pair flanking the Baptistry featuring a guardian angel. Its companion is *Guardian Angel* (Window #6) on the south side of the Baptistry. As modern works of stained glass art, they are in pleasant contrast with the majority of windows that beautify St. Paul's. The liberal use of clear glass in both windows brings in a brighter light allowing the pair to stand out.

The heavenly being is dressed in a red garment and green cloak. The kneeling figure, with a fine set of golden wings, is in an attitude of prayer, with palms together, fingers extended and touching, and head bent.

**SYMBOLISM:** The angel plays various roles: a messenger, artist's muse, companion, and an attendant spirit or guardian.

**MEMORIAL:** There is no memorial nameplate on this window, nor is there one on its companion. Both were given in memory of a three year old child, Roseanne Marie Sawyer, born in 1970 to Mr. and Mrs. William Russell Sawyer. On July 4, 1973, she accidentally fell into a canal where she nearly drowned. Roseanne was rushed to the hospital where she was revived, but died two days later. The child was buried in a ceremony from St. Paul's with Father Gene Norman officiating.

**NOTE:** There are minor variations between this version of the guardian angel and the companion *Guardian Angel.* The windows were originally installed backward and had to be re-installed.

Guardian Angel

# Baptism of Jesus

**Phipps, Ball & Burnham (conjecture)**
**1920**
**79 3/4″ x 27 3/4″**

*In Memory of William Hunt Harris, Jr.*
*Mar. 8, 1904 - June 9, 1906*

**DESCRIPTION:** John the Baptist, clothed in animal skins, is in the act of baptizing Jesus. The water is being poured from a round, shallow bowl. Encircling his shoulders is a banderole with the words "Agnus Dei." Jesus, robed in blue, with downcast eyes and hands crossed over his chest, stands in humility.

**SYMBOLISM:** "Agnus Dei," Latin for "Lamb of God," symbolizes Jesus. John the Baptist was the first to bestow this name upon Jesus, as he said, "Behold the Lamb of God, who taketh away the sins of the world." *(John 1:29)* In the Anglican liturgy, the *Agnus Dei* is sung during communion.

**MEMORIAL:** William Hunt Harris, Jr. was born March 8, 1904. He was the infant son of Mr. and Mrs William Hunt Harris, Sr.. Mr. Harris was born in Louisiana and came to Key West as a 20 year old young man. He studied law, and during the short life of his son, was a senator of the 24th District. He later became a respected judge of the Criminal Court. The infant's mother was Mary Louise Porter Harris, the daughter of Dr. J.Y. Porter, Sr., who was the generous donor of several windows in the church: *Jesse Tree* (Window #102), *Saint Luke* (Window #111) and *Nativity Adoration* (Window #112).

The child was baptized in St. Paul's third church, which was destroyed in the hurricane of 1909. The priest was William Curtis White, Priest in Charge of (First) Holy Innocents. The sponsors were William R. Porter, J. Yates Porter, and Mrs. Mary Harris.

The family lived at 425 Caroline Street. The child's sister, Minnie Porter Harris, and a brother, William Curry Harris, were born after his death.

Baptism of Jesus

# Window #3
# Baptism of Jesus

### (Detail)
### Phipps, Ball & Burnham(Conjecture)

### 1920
### 79 3/4″ x 27 3/4″

### *In Memory of William Hunt Harris, Jr.*
### *Mar. 8, 1904 – June 9, 1906*

**DESCRIPTION:**  In this detail, the artist has succeeded in capturing the strong character and deep emotion at the moment of the baptism of Jesus by his cousin, John the Baptist.  The facial features are well modeled, the golden nimbus and scarlet garment around the shoulders creates a poignant and moving stained glass picture.

**THE STORY:**  John the Baptist was born of an elderly couple descending from the priestly family of Aaron.  Some scholars believe that John went into the desert to live when his parents died; others believe his parents took him to the desert to escape Herod's slaughter of Jewish baby boys.

John was known as the "Baptist" because he preached to his fellow Jews that they should repent and be baptized.  John was a Nazarite, one who pledged to deny himself the luxuries of society and human comforts to demonstrate his love of God.  Following John's baptism of Jesus it is written:

*And with that a voice came from heaven,*
*which said,*
*"This is my beloved son in whom I am well pleased. "*
*(Matthew 3:17)*

Baptism of Jesus
(Detail)

# Jesus Blessing Little Children

**(Detail)**
**Phipps, Ball & Burnham (Conjecture)**
**1920**
**79″ x 27″**

*In Loving Memory of Winona Bocker Long*
*Born December 17, 1911     Died August 13, 1913*

**DESCRIPTION:** In this narrative window, Jesus, simply clothed and unshod, welcomes and embraces the children who have come to him willingly and unabashed.

**SYMBOLISM:** The open-faced flowers, particularly the daisies, are symbols of youth and innocence. The Tri-Radiant Nimbus can be used to represent the Father, the Son, and the Holy Ghost. In this case, it represents Jesus, Son of God.

**MEMORIAL:** Winona Bocker Long was born December 17, 1911.  She was the infant daughter of Osbold (Osbul) S. Long and Rosalie Anna Bocker Long. Osbold was in the furniture business and Superintendent of Pen Casualty Company.  He and Rosalie were married on November 14, 1910.

Winona was baptized on February 22, 1912, by St. Paul's rector, The Reverend Charles S. Stout.  The sponsors were Gertrude L. Bocker, The Reverend Charles S. Stout, Robert Clark and Miss Caroline.

*Suffer the little children to come unto*
*me and forbid them not, for such is*
*the kingdom of heaven.*
*(Luke 18:16)*

# Jesus Blessing Little Children

**(Detail)**

# Window #5
# Phillip and the Ethiopian

**(Detail)**
**Studio Unknown**
**After 1920; before 1950**
**79 1/2" x 27"**

*Pray for the Soul of Charles Fredrick Brookins, Priest*

**DESCRIPTION:** Phillip, dressed in rich and costly vestments, is wearing an elaborate headpiece. One hand is raised; the other is holding a scallop shell filled with water. He is in the act of baptizing a devoutly kneeling Ethiopian. This swarthy, bearded man has humbly crossed his arms over his chest. His saffron garments are in contrast to the vivid colors in this window and shed a rich golden light.

**SYMBOLISM:** The story of Phillip and the Ethiopian from *Acts 8:26-40* is simply a story of the all-inclusiveness of Jesus. While traveling from Jerusalem to Gaza, the apostle Phillip encountered an Ethiopian official who, through a practice common to his position at that time, was a eunuch. Through the Christian rite of baptism, Phillip invited him to become part of God's family, where all are loved and welcomed, regardless of ethnic or religious practices and heritage.

**MEMORIAL:** Charles Frederick Brookins was born in Eaton, Ohio on December 21, 1864. His parents were William Charles Maclay Brookins and May Elizabeth (Cook). He attended Miami University, Oxford, Ohio, and received a Bachelor of Art in 1890. He attended Bexley Hall and became deacon in 1890. He was ordained priest by Bishop Vincent.

Father Brookins was Rector of St. Paul's Church in 1926. The following year, on October 22, 1927, he died in Pensacola. His church service included: Curate, Church of the Advent, Cincinnati, Ohio, 1893; Rector, St. Mary's Church, Cleveland, Ohio, 1894-1900; Vicar, St. Mary's Chapel, Philadelphia, Pa, 1900-1913; Diocean Missionary, Argyle, Scotland, 1913-1914; Chaplain Metropolitan Life Insurance Company's Sanitarium, Mt. McGregor, New York, 1915-1918; Chaplain, Bethany Home, Glendale, Ohio, 1919; St. Thomas, Virgin Islands.

# Phillip and the Ethiopian
**(Detail)**

# Window #6

# Guardian Angel

**Studio Unknown**
**Circa 1975**
**61 1/2″ x 20 1/2″**

*Roseanne Marie Sawyer*
*Born 1970   Died 1973*

**DESCRIPTION:** The window is a companion to *Guardian Angel* (Window #2), one of a pair given in memory of little Roseanne Marie Sawyer.  Although it is a more modern window in artistic style than the majority of the other windows in St. Paul's, it is nonetheless, equally beautiful.  The heavenly being is dressed in a red garment and green cloak, similar to the angel in Window #2.  The golden-winged figure is also kneeling in an attitude of prayer.

However, in this window, the Guardian Angel has hands clasped together in prayer with fingers intertwined rather than with flattened palms and fingers.

**SYMBOLISM:**  It is quite fitting and also poignant that the windows featuring the Guardian Angel, whose role is that of attendant spirit, were given in memory of a small child.  They are positioned so the angel can watch over the entrance to the Baptistry, the place where children first enter the church.

**MEMORIAL:**  Roseanne Marie Sawyer, daughter of Mr. and Mrs. William Russell Sawyer was born in 1970 and died tragically on July 4, 1973, at the age of three, following a fall into a canal.

Guardian Angel

# Moses Smiting the Rock

**Studio Unknown**
**After 1920   Before 1950**
**63 1/4" x 27"**

*In Sacred Memory of Rosana M. Myers*
*Born March 7, 1884   Died Dec. 27, 1920*

**DESCRIPTION:** Moses, the dominant figure, is seen in the act of smiting the rock with his staff. An abundance of water is flowing from the steep rugged cliff. One onlooker appears aghast; others are bent upon filling their containers with the precious fluid.

**THE STORY:** While Israel was encamped in the wilderness, Moses made a serious mistake. Because of a water shortage, people began to quarrel and blamed him for leading them into the wilderness. God had told him to go and speak to the rock and water would flow forth. However, Moses lost his temper and struck the rock in anger. Although water poured forth, by not following God's instructions his actions showed he did not trust God, who decreed that Moses could not bring his people into the promised land and they wandered the wilderness for 40 years.

**MEMORIAL:** At this time, no information about Rosana M. Myers can be found. She is not listed in the census, cemetery records, or St. Paul's records.

Moses Smiting the Rock

Window #7

# Moses Smiting the Rock

**(Detail)**
**Studio Unknown**
**After 1920; before 1950**

*In Sacred Memory of Rosana M. Myers*
*Born March 7, 1884   Died December 27, 1920*

**DESCRIPTION:** This serene girl is wearing a loosely fitted blue garment with a white veil tossed lightly over her head.  She is gathering water in a shallow brass bowl to fill a large pottery jug.

**THE STORY:** If one assumes that this young woman was a daughter, she was expected to help her mother.  At a very early age she began to learn the various domestic skills she would need to become a good wife and mother.  By the age of 12 a young girl had become a homemaker in her own right and was allowed to marry.

Every family needed water which was no easy task to obtain.  Women going to the common well for their families would need considerable strength to carry the heavy jug back to the dwelling place.  However, the trip for water gave them a chance to talk to others, exchange news and gossip.

# Moses Smiting the Rock

**(Detail)**

# Holy Trinity Roundel

**Phipps, Ball & Burnham**
**1920**
**7'2" x 29 1/2"**

*Edith Shackleford  Born 1879  Died 1898*
*James A. Shackleford  Born 1883  Died 1919*

**DESCRIPTION:**  The roundel bearing the Shield of the Trinity is red, bordered in shades of blue.  The shield is gold, with inner and outer circles of white.  The inscription is in Latin.

**SYMBOLISM:**  The Shield of the Trinity is an interesting and expressive design.  It is a joy to beginning Latin students, and a favorite stained glass design of the medieval church.  The shield contains groups of statements indicating positive statements of what each member of the Godhead is, and the others of what they are not.

The center circle contains the word "Deus," the Latin word for God.  The three outer circles contain the words, "Pater," or Father, "Filius," or Son, and "Sanctus Spiritus," or Holy Spirit.  In the bands connecting the center circle to the outer circle is the Latin word "est", or is.  To read the symbol properly, begin in the center circle and go out each band to the connecting outer circle:  "God is Father," "God is Son," and "God is Holy Spirit."

The outer circle is connected by bands with the Latin phrase "no est," or is not.  By connecting the outer circles with the outer band we read:  "The Father is not the Son,"  "The Son is not the Holy Spirit," and "The Holy Spirit is not the Father."

The meaning of this exercise explains the doctrine of the Trinity which holds that God is the Father, the Son and the Holy Spirit; however, the Father, the Son and the Holy Spirit are separate from each other.

**MEMORIAL:**  Edith Shackleford was born in Key West on May 8, 1879, and was baptized at St. Paul's.  Her parents were James R. and Henrietta Shackleford, remembered in the *Saint John Roundel* (Window #9).  She had a number of sisters, and a brother, James.  Little is known about James except his birth.  According to the information on the window, he died in 1919.

The window was probably given by the remaining members of the family: Mrs. George R. English, whose husband was a porter at a local hotel, Lucille Shackleford and Genevieve Shackleford.

Holy Trinity Roundel

# Saint John Roundel

**Phipps, Ball & Burnham**
**1920**
**7'2" x 29 1/2"**

*James R. Shackleford  Born 1851   Died 1906*
*Henrietta Shackleford  Born 1852  Died 1915*

**DESCRIPTION:**  The eagle is set upon a scarlet background encircled with shades of blue.  This handsome bird with outstretched wings is poised for flight.  It sports fine feathers and wonderfully shaped talons.  The head with the golden nimbus is turned to the right; the banderole across the body from wing to wing reads "St. John."

**SYMBOLISM:**  The eagle is the Christian symbol for St. John, the Evangelist.  It is said to represent his desire to reach and spread the highest truths.  It exemplifies power, victory and the spread of the Gospel.

**MEMORIAL:**  James R. Shackleford, a black man, was born in Missouri on April 8, 1851.  He came to Key West sometime prior to 1874, worked as a carpenter and later operated a grocery store in the 800 block of Duval Street.

Henrietta Delaney was born in March 1852 in Florida.  She and James were married on June 7, 1874, by The Reverend John Reuter, rector of St. Paul's.

The census for 1900 states they were parents of nine children, five still alive at that time.  The following were baptized: Mary, Julia, Edith, Elizabeth, James, Marquery, Eugenia, and Genevieve.

James R. Shackleford died in 1906; Henrietta in 1915.  Two of their children, James and Edith, are remembered in *Holy Trinity Roundel* (Window #8).

Saint John Roundel

# Pomegranate Roundel

**Phipps, Ball & Burnham**
**1920**
**7'2" x 29 1/2"**

*Drucilla Duke Williams*
*May 11, 1827 – December 21, 1907*

**DESCRIPTION:** The white pomegranate contrasted against a vivid background and encircled with shades of blue is fringed with leaves. It has often been mistaken for other symbols. However, the central shape is that of a pomegranate, and it appears to be bursting. The surrounding leaves appear to be palm fronds.

**SYMBOLISM:** This roundel is possibly a dual symbol. The bursting pomegranate is a symbol of immortality, hope and the Resurrection; the palm leaf is a sign of victory and heavenly rewards.

**MEMORIAL:** Drucilla Duke Williams was born in Alabama on May 11, 1827. Her parents were Reason and Jane Duke. The family moved to Florida, where they farmed land about three miles up the Miami River. In January 1836, when Drucilla was a small child, the family fled the Cape Florida Lighthouse, which marked the southern tip of the island which is now Key Biscayne, for protection against Indian attack.

In 1843, the same year that her father became the lighthouse keeper at Cape Florida, Drucilla, at age16, married Franklin D. Phillips, but was soon widowed.

On October 22, 1846, Drucilla, now 19, married Cortland P. Williams, a Coast Pilot in Key West, remembered in the next window, *Mitre Roundel* (Window #11).

Pomegranate Roundel

# Mitre Roundel

**Phipps, Ball & Burnham**
**1920**
**7'2" x 29 1/2"**

*Courtland Parker Williams*
*Born September 11, 1825   Died October 6, 1892*

**DESCRIPTION:** The mitre, a liturgical headdress, is set upon a scarlet background encircled with shades of blue. It is ornate and appears to be embellished with embroidery and jewels. On either side is a crosier, or pastoral staff, shaped like a shepherd's crook. On the lappets are four Maltese crosses, formed by four spearheads touching at the center. At the top of the mitre is a larger Maltese cross.

**SYMBOLISM:** In Biblical times, the mitre was the official headdress of the high priest. It was made of fine linen and had a total length of about eight yards. Today it is the folding cap representing the cloven tongues of fire on Pentecost worn by archbishops, bishops and abbots as a symbol of authority. The crosier is also a symbol of office carried by bishops and abbots. The Maltese Cross dates back to the days of the Crusades when the order of the Hospitallers used it as their emblem. Later they made their headquarters on the island of Malta.

**MEMORIAL:** Courtland Parker Williams, son of William Earl Williams and Eliza Vial Appleby Williams was born in Rhode Island. In the 1880 census he is listed as a Coast Pilot, an important position in the maritime history of Key West.

Since the early history of Florida and Key West, local pilots were engaged to help ships navigate the sometimes treacherous coast to ensure maximum safety. Florida began licensing coast pilots in 1839, and the first comprehensive statutes guiding the service were written in 1868. Prior to the licensing of the profession, the business was often a highly competitive race to the sea.

Courtland married Drucilla Duke, daughter of a lighthouse keeper at Cape Florida, who was born on May 11, 1827 in Alabama. Their children, Bertha, Buelah, and Blanche were all born in Florida. They had an adopted son, Thomas Whitehurst.

It is possible that two of their married children, Mrs. George W. Reynolds and Mrs. H. B. Boyer might be the donors of this window honoring their father, and of *Pomegranate Roundel* (Window #10), in memory of Drucilla Duke Williams, their mother.

Mitre Roundel

# Holy Spirit Roundel

**Phipps, Ball & Burnham**
**1920**
**7'2" x 29 1/2"**

### *Gift of St. Paul's Flower Guild*

**DESCRIPTION:** The scarlet roundel encircled with shades of blue contains a white dove. Surrounding the head is a nimbus, a circle of radiant light. The inscription beneath this symbol is "Sanctus Spiritus."

**SYMBOLISM:** The dove is the symbol for the Holy Spirit and "Sanctus Spiritus" is Latin for the Holy Spirit.

**MEMORIAL:** Both *Holy Spirit Roundel* and *Agnus Dei Roundel* (Window #13) were given to St. Paul's by the Flower Guild. When the window was donated there must have been a separate organization for the procurement and arrangement of flowers. Today, the Flower Guild takes that responsibility. In the early years of St. Paul's, the members could not easily obtain flowers relying only on flowers were grown in gardens on the island. The Rock Rose was a favorite, as well as the small red carnation.

The best example of the work of the Flower Guild is shown in a rare photograph of St. Paul's third church. It features the church decorated for the wedding of Key West's beloved physician, Joseph N. Fogarty, and his bride, Corrine Curry. The wedding took place on January 16, 1900, and the church was lavishly decorated with ferns, flowers and palm fronds. The popular couple said their vows beneath a white bell, but one cannot discern from the photograph if this was fashioned from flowers. One elderly church member born this same year remembers the "old folks" remarking that, "Dr. Fogarty was married under the bell."

*Third Church 1888-1909.*
*The church is decorated for the 1900 Curry-Fogarty wedding.*

Holy Spirit Roundel

# Agnus Dei Roundel

**Phipps, Ball & Burnham**
**1920**
**7'2" x 29 1/2"**

### *Gift of St. Paul's Flower Guild*

**DESCRIPTION:** The ruby roundel encircled with shades of blue contains a lamb reclining on a book of seven seals. The lamb carries a white banner with the words "Agnus Dei," Latin for the Lamb of God.

**SYMBOLISM:** The reclining lamb represents Christ, as the "Lamb of God that taketh away the sins of the world." As described in *Revelation 5*, the book represents a scroll, interpreted here as the Bible; the seven seals symbolize the difficulty in opening the book as only Christ can open the seals. In Anglican worship, the "Agnus Dei" or Lamb of God is sung during Communion.

**MEMORIAL:** As was *Holy Spirit Roundel* (Window #12), the *Agnus Dei Roundel* was given to St. Paul's by the Flower Guild, at a time when the Flower Guild and Altar Guild were two separate and distinct organizations.

In the early 1900s, flowers could not be procured from a distant city or florist shop. They came from what was individually grown in private gardens on the island. While The Reverend Gilbert Higgs was rector, he laid out an ornamental garden on the church grounds. One of the showplaces of the city, it featured was a lovely pond by the Guild Hall and water tower where he and Mrs. Higgs would serve tea to their friends in the afternoon.

As young man, Eugene Lowe, son of John Lowe, Jr., who later was to become Dr. Lowe, would gather roses from this garden and go door to door selling them. A lovely brass processional cross was purchased for the church from these sales, and is still in use today. It is presumed that Eugene Lowe's entrepreneurship was promoted by the Flower Guild.

The Guild Hall and water tower have long since disappeared, replaced by a well-kept and serene Memorial Garden.

Many ladies have been responsible for the decoration of the church and altar. Among them was Miss Leila Pitcher, a devout communicant, who taught members a reverence for their work that is rare in today's busy world. Well-remembered are the matchless altar arrangements made by Betty Henriquez Collins and Louise Lee.

Agnus Dei Roundel

# Presentation of Jesus in the Temple

**Studio Unknown**
**After 1920 – Before 1950**
**68 1/2″ x 23 1/4″**

*In Loving Memory of Josephine Ximenez Rawson*
*Born October 12, 1835 – Died April 10, 1922*

**DESCRIPTION:** In this detail of the narrative window, Mary is shown in an attitude of prayer. Over her blonde hair she wears a head covering. Her free-flowing garments are ornamented at the neck and sleeves; over these is a sapphire blue cloak. Her head is uplifted, her face serene, and the halo is ruby. On close inspection, the flesh tones and light colored garments have a slightly greenish tint.

**THE STORY:** Mary has come to the temple with Joseph and Jesus for purification. This was a requirement of Jewish women 40 days after the birth of a boy child: "Every male that openeth the womb shall be called holy to the Lord." (*Luke 2:24*)

**MEMORIAL:** Josephine, daughter of Joseph and Magdalena Ximenez, was born in Florida. Her father was a well-to-do mariner, whose wealth was derived from the lucrative shipping industry so predominant in Key West at the time.

Josephine was educated at Miss Edwards' school in New Haven, Connecticut. When she returned to Key West, she took an active part in the work of St. Paul's Church as a Sunday school teacher and assistant to the organist, Mary Ann Porter. When Mary Ann died in 1860, Josephine became St. Paul's second organist and served 25 years without compensation. Outside of church work, she taught in a school for girls.

In 1875 at the age of 39, Josephine married Edward B. Rawson, formerly of New York. As a cigar manufacturer, Rawson was engaged in a business which diversified the maritime economy and the culture of the island. With the start of the Cuban civil war in 1868, the tobacco industry gradually moved to Key West, becoming a large and vital industry leading to prosperity for the entire population on the small island.

There were no children from the marriage of Josephine and Edward. He died in 1900; she in 1922 at the age of 86.

Presentation of Jesus in the Temple

# Window #15
# Chi Rho Rondel

**Phipps, Ball & Burnham**
**1920**
**7'2 1/2" x 39"**

*John W. Allen*

**DESCRIPTION:** This monogram is a form of the Chi Rho, a symbol for Christ. The upright letter is a combination of a cross and a "P," signifying the first two letters Chi (X) and Rho (P) of the Greek word for Christ, "Christos." They were put together to form this symbol for Christ. The "N" stands for NIKA, or conqueror, in Greek.

**SYMBOLISM:** This adaptation of the Chi Rho symbol stands for Christ the Victor. As a sign of our Lord's victory, the upright Chi Rho was placed in the letter "N."

**MEMORIAL:** John W. Allen was born in Homer, New York on June 11, 1858, the son of William S. and Mary (Sprague) Allen. On August 2, 1886, John married Cornelia M. Pierce, daughter of Lewis and Sarah Pierce who are remembered in *Chalice Roundel* (Window #16).

At 21, John became assistant lighthouse keeper at Alligator Reef, off Islamorada. He held a number of positions during his lifetime: Collector of Revenue, director of the First National Bank, and was also in the furniture business.

In 1900 he lived at 700 Fleming Street, at or near the present site of the Monroe County Library. John died on March 24, 1918. His brother, George Whiting Allen, is remembered in *Christ Among the Doctors* (Window #108).

Chi Rho Roundel

# Chalice Roundel

**Phipps, Ball & Burnham**
**1920**
**7'2 1/2" x 39"**

*Sarah J. Pierce*
*Lewis E. Pierce*

**DESCRIPTION:** A chalice with a host suspended just above the rim is encircled with the words "Sanctus, Sanctus." On the host are the letters "IHS."

**SYMBOLISM:** This roundel represents the Bread and Wine of the Lord's Supper. The word chalice is Latin for cup or goblet. The goblet is the classical style used to administer the wine at Holy Communion. "Sanctus" is Latin for Holy. The letters "IHS" on the host, or Eucharistic bread, above the chalice is a monogram representing Christ. "IHS" are the first three letters (iota, eta, sigma ) of the Greek spelling of Jesus, and is the way Christ's name was spelled in the Middle Ages.

**MEMORIAL:** The window was given in memory of Sarah J. Pierce and Lewis E. Pierce. Lewis E. Pierce, 25, married Sarah Jane Albrey, 19, on June 23, 1848 in Key West. Both bride and groom were born in the Bahamas.

In the 1860 census, Lewis is listed as a ship's carpenter and Sarah as a seamstress. In the 1870 census the children living in the home were Lydia, Charles, Albert, Amelia (Cornelia) and Anna. Lewis E. Pierce, Jr. is not mentioned as he was probably living elsewhere.

During the Civil War, Lewis E. Pierce, Sr. and his son, Lewis E. Pierce, Jr., are listed as members of the Union Volunteer Corps. This must have led to interesting discussions, if not tensions. According to Stan Windhorn and Wright Langley in *Yesterday's Key West*, although the island was occupied by a Union army garrison and was the site of a major Union naval base during the Civil War, a majority its citizens were secessionists in their sympathies.

In his book, *Key West the Old and the New*, Jefferson B. Browne writes that "Young" Lewey Pierce was an accepted champion with his fist and "is now a sedate retired capitalist at Miami."

The *Chi Rho Roundel* (Windows #15) and *Alpha and Omega Roundel* (Window #17) are also dedicated to family members related by blood or marriage. Together with *Chalice Roundel*, the three comprise a single window on the lower level of the south transept.

Chalice Roundel

# Window #17
# Alpha and Omega Roundel

**Phipps, Ball & Burnham**
**1920**
**7' 2 1/2" x 39"**

*Lewis H. Moss*
*Joseph H. Moss*

**DESCRIPTION:** The red roundel encircled with shades of blue holds the monogram of the Greek letters Alpha, in yellow and Omega, in white.

**SYMBOLISM:** Alpha (A) and Omega (Ω) are the first and last letters of the Greek alphabet and signify that Jesus is the beginning and the end of all things: "the First and the Last." Alpha and Omega is an early symbol representing Christ and has been found in the catacombs, on Christian signet rings, on post-Constantine coins and on mosaics of ancient churches.

**MEMORIAL:** The window is dedicated to a father and son. Joseph H. Moss was born in the Bahamas in 1846, and worked in Key West as a carpenter. On February 15, 1873, he married Lydia E. Pierce, daughter of Lewis E. Pierce and Sarah Jane Albrey Pierce *Chalice Roundel* (Window #16). Lydia was born circa 1853 and was about 20 at the time of her marriage; the groom was about 27. The wedding was performed by Charles A. Gilbert, rector of St. Paul's.

Joseph died prior to 1900; Lydia lived on for many years. She was a teacher at Sears school and listed herself as Head of Household in the 1900 census after her husband's death.

Their son, Lewis H. Moss, was born in 1873 or 1874 in Key West. He was Deputy Collector of Customs, and lived at 700 Fleming Street, the site of the present Monroe County Library. On April 8, 1904 he married Mary Baldwin. The ceremony was performed by The Reverend A. B. Friend, S. J. of the Roman Catholic Church. Lewis died on June 1, 1917.

The *Chi Rho Roundel* (Windows #15) and *Chalice Roundel* (Window #16) are also dedicated to family members related by blood or marriage and make up a single window in the lower level of the south transept.

Alpha and Omega Roundel

# Window #18
# The Annunciation of Our Lady

### Phipps, Ball & Burnham
### 1920
### 68" x 23 1/2"

### *Memorial Daughters of the King*

**DESCRIPTION:**  Located by the Lady Chapel in the south transept, this window is a small but beautiful one, in keeping with the rule of life of prayer and service of the donors, the Daughters of the King.  The archangel Gabriel, dressed in a loose, flowing robe, appears as a handsome youth.  His head is encircled with a radiant light and above this nimbus a sweep of glorious red wings is seen.  Holding a golden scepter in his right hand and with the left hand outstretched, he is telling Mary that she has been chosen to give birth to the Messiah.

**SYMBOLISM:** The golden scepter is a symbol of authority.  The dove and the rays of light shining on Mary represent the Holy Spirit and the words spoken by the angel: "The Holy Spirit will come on you and the power of the Most High will overshadow you.  Therefore also the holy one who is born from you will be called the Son of God." (*Luke 1:35*)  The lilies represent Mary's purity.

**MEMORIAL:**  The Daughters of the King was founded in 1885 as a lay order for women in the Episcopal Church.  Similar to monastic orders, the Daughters of the King have a rule of life of prayer and service.

Information about the early order was provided by Mrs. Emma Watson Fraga prior to 1958, or was found in Browne's *Key West, The Old and the New*.  The Daughters of the King chapter of St. Paul's, No. 427, received its charter on May 21, 1895.  It is believed that Mary Nieves Brown or Josephine Rawson was the first president.  There were at least 12 charter members and it is thought they included the following: Josephine Ximenez Rawson (Mrs. Edward B.), Clara Hertell Higgs (Mrs. Gilbert Higgs) , Mary A. Johnson, Roagie Allen, Emeline Susan "Emma" Watson, Melvena (Mellie) Bethel and Elizabeth (Lillie) Watlington.

A number of these charter members were active in procuring funds to have the window installed in the present church.  The documentary information on the window was found quite by accident on yellowed pages of records being placed in a safe, solving the mystery of one of the several unsigned windows.  Entries on the fragmented pages state that as early as 1917 the Elks donated $10 to the Daughters for their memorial window to be placed in the new building. From September 1919 to March 10, 1920, there was a detailed list of members and the amount of money they donated to each window:  Mrs. Harriet Babcock gave a social at which punch was served; Mary Nieves Bethel gave a supper at her home and served ice cream for dessert.  No mention of the window was found after June 1920.

The Annunciation of Our Lady

# The Annunciation of Our Lady

(Detail #1 and Detail #2)

**MOTTO OF THE ORDER OF THE DAUGHTERS OF THE KING**
*For His Sake*
*I am one: but I am one*
*I cannot do everything: but I can do something.*
*What I can do, I ought to do.*
*What I ought to do, by the grace of God, I will do.*
*Lord, what wilt Thou have me to do?*

For the purpose of this book, Lucy Knowles has been chosen to represent the group of the Daughters of the King in 1919-1920 who contributed to the purchase of the window. Her story provides a glimpse into the lives of the people of Key West of that time.

Lucy was born on January 6, 1862 at Northend, Long Island, Bahamas, a former cotton plantation, undoubtedly the remnants of the efforts of the Loyalist, American colonists who supported the crown and chose to leave the Carolinas during the war of the American Revolution to settle in the Bahamas.

Lucy's father was Clement Knowles; her mother, Julia Rahming Knowles. The entire family came to live in Key West in the 1890s. Her brother, Clement, had a cigar factory on Fitzpatrick Street and many of the family members worked in this industry.

As there was no school for girls on Long Island, Bahamas, Lucy learned to read and write at her mother's knee. She became an avid reader and was much in demand in Key West as a letter writer for those who were in need of proper written communication.

Although she never married, there is a romantic letter in St. Paul's archives written by a supply priest, but Lucy's state of health closed the door to marriage. She was a lady, prim and proper, well-loved and well-remembered. Lucy was a member of the Altar Guild, Sunday school teacher, and a Daughter of the King. She entered an Episcopal Home in Brooklyn, New York where she died an octogenarian in 1943.

There is also an oft repeated tale of a Daughter named Lucy that offers a description of an experience in the disastrous hurricane of 1909 that destroyed many of the churches in Key West, including St. Paul's. During the storm, this Daughter apparently forgot the order's rule of prayer. With the threat of the on-coming hurricane, the men of the home had left hurriedly to secure the cigar factory and the all-important tobacco. That left two maiden aunts and one young girl, Amy, at home. When the roof of the house threatened to blow away, the three sought shelter in a downstairs room. As the water rose, they sat on the piano. For a time young Amy held a treasured bowl of goldfish over her head, but when the tidal action began to move the piano, she was terrified and called to her aunt: "Lucy, Lucy, pray for me!" Lucy's reply was short and swift: "Pray for yourself. Every pot sits on its own bottom!"

Detail #1

Detail #2

# The Annunciation of Our Lady

# Window #19
# Raising Jairus' Daughter

**Phipps, Ball & Burnham (conjecture)**
**1920 or before 1950**

*In Memory of Blanche Stanhope Reynolds*
*Born Aug. 26, 1862 – Oct. 7, 1918*

**DESCRIPTION:** In the window a man, a woman and Jesus are standing beside the bedside of a young girl. Jesus is holding the child's right hand in his. His left hand is upraised.

**THE STORY:** The window depicts one of Jesus' miracles as told in the New Testament Gospels. It tells of Jairus, one of the leaders of the synagogue, who implored Jesus to come to his home and lay His hands on his little daughter that she might recover from her serious illness. Before they reached the house, it was reported that she was dead. Jesus said to Jairus, "Do not fear, only believe." Taking her by the hand He said to her, "Little girl, I say to you, arise," and immediately the girl got up and walked. (*Mark 5:41-42*)

**MEMORIAL:** Blanche Stanhope Reynolds, nee Williams, was the daughter of Cortland Parker Williams, remembered in the *Mitre Roundel* (Window #11) and Drucilla Duke Williams, remembered in the *Pomegranate Roundel* (Window #10). Blanche was born in Key West on August 26, 1862 and in February 1883 married George W. Reynolds, cigar maker, lawyer, and Clerk of the Circuit Court from 1893 to 1905. Their children were William, Joseph, Clara, one child who died in infancy, and an adopted daughter, Natalie.

George Reynolds designed and built a lovely large home for Blanche on the corner of Flagler Avenue and Reynolds Street. He is remembered in *Saint Matthew* (Window #123).

Raising Jairus' Daughter

# Raising Jairus' Daughter

**(Detail #1)**
**Phipps, Ball & Burnham (conjecture)**
**1920 or before 1950**

*In Memory of Blanche Stanhope Reynolds*
*Born Aug. 26, 1862- Oct. 7, 1918*

**DESCRIPTION:** While the entire window illustrates the raising of Jairus' daughter, this detail depicts the moment when Jesus took the daughter by the hand and said to her, "Little girl, I say to you, arise." *(Mark 5:41)*

The hand of Jesus is in the traditional manner of blessing. The child's hand is bent at the wrist.

This detail illustrates a familiar verse:

*I said to the man who stood at the gate of the years,*
*"Give me light, that I may tread safely into the unknown."*
*And he replied,*
*"Go out into the darkness,*
*Put your hand into the Hand of God.*
*That shall be to you better than light*
*And safer than the known way."*
*The Gate of the Year - Minnie Louis Haskins 1908*

# Raising Jairus' Daughter
**(Detail #1)**

# Chi Rho Roundel

**Phipps, Ball & Burnham**
**1920**
**7′ 3″ x 39″**

### *To the Glory of God*

**DESCRIPTION:** The roundel contains the familiar version of the Chi Rho symbol in white glass against a red background. Each of the arms and the center of the emblem contains golden nail heads. On either side of the Chi Rho is a golden fleur-de-lis.

**SYMBOLISM:** The Chi Rho is a monogram symbolizing Christ. It is comprised of the first two Greek letters, Chi (X) and Rho (P) of the title "Christos." These were eventually put together to form this symbol for Christ. The fleur-de-lis is the conventional form of the lily representing immortality as expressed in the Trinity.

**THE STORY:** As Constantine (272 A. D. – 337 A.D.) was about to go into battle with Maxentius in 312 A. D., he decided to pray to the Son of God although he was not a Christian. While praying, a vision of the Lord, holding the Chi Rho in His hand appeared, and a voice said: "In hoc signo vinces," (In this sign thou shalt conquer). Constantine placed this emblem upon the shields and standards of the Roman legion. The battle was won, and in time Constantine became the first Christian Roman Emperor.

**MEMORIAL:** The donor is not known. The window simply states: *To the Glory of God*.

Chi Rho Roundel

# Window #21
# Saint Matthew Roundel

**Phipps, Ball & Burnham**
**7' 3" x 39"**

*In Loving Memory of*
*Walter James Lightbourne*
*Oct. 13, 1882 – June 30, 1916*

**DESCRIPTION:** The ruby roundel, encircled with blue, green and purple, contains a winged figure of a man dressed in white holding a banderole which reads, "S. Matthew." The nimbus, wings and banderole are golden. Unfortunately, the roundel is cracked.

**SYMBOLISM:** The winged man represents Saint Matthew because he began his gospel with the human genealogy of Jesus. Originally a tax collector, Matthew was called by Jesus to become one of his disciples.

**MEMORIAL:** Walter James Lightbourne was born in Key West on October 13, 1882. He was the son of Walter S. and Florida Lofton Lightbourne. His father was vice president and manager of Cortez Cigar Company which at one time employed 300 men. *The Key West City Directory*, in 1906-1907, lists Walter James as assistant manger of the Cortez Cigar Factory.

He was married on November 8, 1904 to Nellie Moss. James J. Cameron, rector of St. Paul's performed the ceremony with Charles Curry and Benjamin Trevor as witnesses. Walter James and Nellie's children were Walter S., Florida Elmer (Evans), Alice Mary (Carbonell), and Catherine (Demeritt). Following Walter James' death, his widow married Dexter Dorgan.

Saint Matthew Roundel

## Window #22

# IHS Roundel

**Phipps, Ball & Burnham**
**1920**
**7'3" x 39"**

*Lena Victoria Baker*
*Born Sept. 14, 1846   Died June 18, 1908*

**DESCRIPTION:**  The IHS monogram is contrasted against a ruby background and encircled with shades of blue and green. The golden "I" of the monogram is in the shape of a Latin cross with tre-foil ends. The "H" and "S" are of white glass enhanced with a simple design.

**SYMBOLISM:** One of the most familiar monograms as a symbol for Jesus, the IHS is of a later date than the Chi Rho monogram.  Dating from the 8th century, it is derived from the first three letters of the Greek spelling for Jesus, iota, eta, sigma.  It evolved into an abbreviation for "IHEUS," the way Christ's name was spelled in the Middle Ages.  The monogram was used by St. Ignatius of Loyola as a symbol for the Jesuit Order.

**MEMORIAL:** Little is known of Lena Victoria Baker, born in the Bahamas on September 14, 1846. Although a review was made of all available records, only St. Paul's burial records and the cemetery listed her.  Lena Victoria never married; she died on June 18, 1908 and was buried in Key West.

IHS Roundel

# Christ with the Woman of Samaria

**Studio Unknown**
**After 1920   Before 1950**
**68 1/2″ x 23″**

*In Loving Memory of Mellie Bethel*
*Born November 17, 1839*
*Died March 9, 1921*

**DESCRIPTION:** Christ is seated near Jacob's well,  clothed in a red garment with a white head covering and a white gold trimmed cloak over His shoulders.  The right hand is raised in blessing; the left outstretched. A woman stands near Him with a heavy, empty pottery jug balanced on her head.  She is wearing an ornamented blue dress and a scarlet cape over her shoulders.  A white covering almost hides her blonde hair. Bracelets on both arms complete the ensemble.

**THE STORY:**  As told in *John 4:1-38*, after a long walk, Jesus rested at Jacob's well on the outskirts of the village of Sychar.  It was noontime, during the extreme heat of the day and His solitude was broken by a Samaritan woman who came to draw water.  The woman was alone as she was not of good repute and avoided the well in early morning or evening, a time when it would be thronged by all the women of the village who did not want anything to do with her because of her loose living.  Jesus, who was thirsty and had no way of reaching the cool well water, asked the woman for a drink.  The request surprised the shunned woman, however, after some dialogue, she began to see that she was in a great presence.  To this simple, lone woman who questioned Him about the advent of the Messiah, Jesus revealed, "I that speak unto thee am He." (*John 4:26*)

**MEMORIAL:**  Melvina (Mellie) Bethel was born in the Bahamas on November 17,1839.  She was the daughter of Mr. and Mrs. Winer Bethel.  The family came to live in Key West around 1848.  In 1865 she joined the faculty of a school operated by her aunt, Euphemia Lightbourne.  After Euphemia died, Mellie continued to teach and operate the school until 1911.  When the school closed, she taught young girls all types of fancy work (needlework) for 25 cents a week, at times serving cookies and refreshments.  She took loving care of the girls and if there was a downpour, much to the girls' delight, she called a carriage for them.

In 1900 Mellie lived with her brother, Livingston, and his family at 421 Duval Street, in the same block as St. Paul's Church.  The large two-story white house with green trim was ornamented with gingerbread, the adornment of Victorian architecture popular in Key West at that time.

This window is a study in contrasts between its subject and its donor: the woman of Samaria had five husbands; Mellie never married.

Christ with the Woman of Samaria

# Cross and Crown Roundel

**Phipps, Ball & Burnham**
**1920**
**7'2" x 29 1/2"**

*Emma V. Brightman*
*Born Oct. 14   1863*
*Died April 16   1892*

**DESCRIPTION:**  The scarlet roundel encircled with shades of blue contains a golden crown; within the crown is a cross.  The artist chose a Latin budded cross with trefoil ends representing the Holy Trinity.  The crown has flowing lines ending with stylized fleur de lis and decorated with other artistic geometric embellishments.

**SYMBOLISM:** The cross and crown together symbolize the reward for the faithful: life after death.

*"Be thou faithful unto death*
*and I will give thee a*
*Crown of Life."*
*(Revelation 2:10)*

**MEMORIAL:** Emma V. Roberts was born October 14, 1863.  She was married to George Henry Brightman on January 3, 1881 in a ceremony performed by The Reverend Juan B. Baez, provisional rector of St. Paul's.  George Ferguson, next door neighbor to the groom, was one of the witnesses.

George Henry Brightman was born circa 1856 in Florida of parents from Connecticut.  Emma and George had two children, Mary T., born October 24, 1881, and Lillian, born September 9, 1886. Unfortunately, Emma died in Philadelphia on April 16, 1892 at the age of 29 of a dread disease and was buried in Key West.

Cross and Crown Roundel

# Chalice and Cruets Roundel

**Phipps, Ball & Burnham Roundel**
**1920**
**7'2" x 29 1/2"**

*To John J. Warren*
*Emma E. Warren*
*Edgar L. Warren*

**DESCRIPTION:** The roundel is red, bordered in shades of blue and green. The chalice is a golden goblet decorated with a banded design near the top. The knob is simply decorated and the stem has outward curving lines ornamented with double lines ending with a scalloped foot. The goblet sits on a golden paten. On either side are cruets of white glass topped with Latin crosses.

**SYMBOLISM:** These vessels represent the Sacrament of Holy Communion. The chalice holds the wine mixed with water for consecration. The paten is the plate that holds the bread. The cruets, one for wine and one for water, are used for preparing the chalice before the prayer of consecration.

**MEMORIAL:** John J. Warren was born on May 24, 1845 in Florida, was baptized at St. Paul's, and married Emma E. Moss, born in the Bahamas in 1848. John and Emma were married on July 1, 1864 by The Reverend Osgood Herrick, rector of St. Paul's.

By the 1880 census they were the parents of five children: Ellen, John M., William E., Edgar and John H. At this time John J. was working as a watchman for the Navy and the family lived on Olivia Street.

At the turn of the century Emma and John J. had moved to Dey Street and lived with their daughter, Ellen, her husband, Edward Lowe, and grandson, Eugene. Their daughter, Sadie L., born between 1880 and 1900, also resided there, and John continued his work as a watchman.

Their son, Edgar L. Warren, also remembered in this window, was born in 1873. He died at the young age of 17 on July 26, 1890 in St. Augustine, Florida and was buried in Key West.

Chalice and Cruets Roundel

# Saint Luke Roundel

**Phipps, Ball & Burnham**
**1920**
**7'2" x 29 1/2"**

*Ellen E. Filer*

**DESCRIPTION:** The ruby roundel encircled with shades of blue contains a gentle-looking, smiling ox with golden wings. Over the head is a nimbus or circle of radiant light. The tail curves upward and one foreleg is elevated. Beneath the body is a banderole identifying the winged creature as Saint Luke.

**SYMBOLISM:** The winged ox is the symbolic representation of Luke. The ox, or animal of sacrifice, is a fitting representation since Luke's gospel stresses the sacrifice, priesthood, and atonement of Jesus.

**MEMORIAL:** Ellen E. Bartlum, daughter of Joseph and Mary Ellen Lowe Bartlum, was born in Green Turtle Cay, Bahamas in 1842. Her uncle, John Bartlum, built a large schooner, *Euphemia*, named for Euphemia Curry, remembered in the *Ascension, Pentecost, Resurrection* (Window #122). Uncle John also built a clipper ship, the *Stephen B. Mallory*, 1000 tons burden, a venture never before attempted in a southern shipyard. When the *Stephen R. Mallory,* carrying a life-sized figurehead of her well-known namesake on her bow, was launched in Key West in 1856, Ellen was 14, and probably was aware of the pride and the excitement felt in the city.

Ellen was married on May 9, 1859 in Key West to Samuel Filer, a well-to-do lumber merchant. They were the parents of Ellen Elizabeth, born in Key West on June 7, 1868.

Ellen E. Filer died at the age of 68, in 1910, and was buried in the Filer plot in the Key West cemetery. Samuel died on October 15, 1922.

This window is a companion to the next window, *Font Roundel* (Window #27), also given in memory of Ellen E. Filer.

Saint Luke Roundel

# Font Roundel

**Phipps, Ball & Burnham**
**1920**
**7'2" x 29 1/2"**

*Ellen E. Filer*

**DESCRIPTION:** The ruby roundel encircled with shades of blue and lavender contains a covered octagonal baptismal font. On one side of the font is a golden flagon; on the other side is a closed Bible or Gospel Book with the letters, IHS, on the cover.

**SYMBOLISM:** All the articles in this roundel pertain to the Sacrament of Holy Baptism. The person baptized becomes a Christian, a child of God, an inheritor of the kingdom of heaven. The IHS on the Bible is a monogram representing the Greek word for Jesus, derived from iota, eta, sigma, the first three letters of the Greek spelling for Jesus.

**MEMORIAL:** This window is a companion to *Saint Luke Roundel* (Window #26), both given in memory of Ellen E. Filer, presumably by her husband, Samuel, and daughter, Ellen Elizabeth. Young Ellen, "Bessie," married George Babcock on November 19, 1890. George owned a grocery store and served as mayor of Key West. Ellen Babcock lived for 87 years. She died in October 1955 and was buried by The Reverend John Armfield, rector of St. Paul's.

Font Roundel

# Window #28
# Saint Mark Roundel

**Phipps, Ball & Burnham**
**1920**
**7'2" x 29 1/2"**

### *In Memory of William H. Williams*

**DESCRIPTION:** This ruby roundel encircled with shades of blue contains a white lion with golden wings. The head has a nimbus or circle of holy light. The tail swings upward and one foreleg is slightly raised. The banderole beneath the lion's body identifies the winged creature as Saint Mark.

**SYMBOLISM:** The lion, king of the beasts, was a figure of resurrection in early times. It is an appropriate symbol for Saint Mark, whose writings dwell upon Christ's Resurrection. "The voice of one crying in the wilderness," (*Mark 1:3*) the beginning words of his gospel, suggests the roar of a lion.

**MEMORIAL:** William H. Williams, born in 1853, married Nellie Blanche Lowe on November 9, 1880. The ceremony was performed by The Reverend Juan B. Baez, rector of St. Paul's. Samuel Lowe and William Runiel were the witnesses.

In 1900, William was the city treasurer and lived at 508 Duval Street. He died March 9, 1904 and is buried in the Key West Cemetery.

Saint Mark Roundel

# Window #29
# Cross and Anchor Roundel

**Phipps, Ball & Burnham**
**1920**

*In Loving Memory of Mother*
*Elvera Elizabeth Weatherford*
*Nearer My God to Thee*

**DESCRIPTION:** The scarlet roundel encircled with shades of blue contains an anchor with a golden Latin cross securely tied to it by a knotted rope. There is a fleur-de-lis between the anchor and the cross.

**SYMBOLISM:** The anchor, the symbol of hope, used together with a cross stands for the hope of eternal life. The Anchor Cross was used by the early Christians in the catacombs. The fleur-de-lis is the conventional form of a lily, the flower representing immortality.

**MEMORIAL:** Elvera (Elvira) Elizabeth Johnson was born in Florida in 1852 or 1853. Her father was born in New Jersey and her mother in New Hampshire. On December 31, 1871, she married Julius Augustus Weatherford, with The Reverend Sam C. Craft of the Baptist Church officiating. Julius was born in 1849 in Florida of parents born in the Bahamas.

By 1900, Elvira and Julius were the parents of three living children: Pressie L., 27, and Margarette, 9. The third child was not living at home at the time. Elizabeth Johnson, Elvira's mother, was also a member of the household living at 629 Caroline Street. At that time Julius worked as a painter.

Apparently, Elvira did not use her first name. On the marriage license she is listed as Lizzie; in the census she is listed as Elizabeth; at her death the priest recorded her as Aloira; and, Phipps, Ball & Burnham used Elvera for the glass window.

Elvira Elizabeth Weatherford died November 14, 1919 and was buried by The Reverend Stout of St. Paul's.

Cross and Anchor Roundel

# Genealogy Window-Prophets Isaiah and Jeremiah

**Charles Connick Associates**
**1959**
**9' 8 1/2" x 29 1/2"**

*To the Glory of God and in Memory of*
*Eric Curry   1894 – 1956*
*Given by his Mother*

**DESCRIPTION:** Viewed as a single splendid unit, *Jesse Tree* (Window #102), installed in 1920 by Phipps, Ball & Burnham, and the flanking *Prophet* windows (#101 and #103) installed in 1959 by Connick Associates, depict the Messianic prophesies of the Old Testament. Connick Associates brought together such continuity with the earlier Phipps, Ball & Burnham window that, at first glance, one does not realize that they were made at different times by different studios.

In this right panel *Prophet* window, two of the four major prophets of Israel, Isaiah and Jeremiah are depicted. The other two prophets, Daniel and Ezekiel, are featured in *Genealogy Window-Prophets Daniel and Ezekiel*, on the left side of *Jesse Tree*.

The top figure, Isaiah, stands barefoot, holding a rose in one hand and a scroll in the other. His layered garments are colorful: the outer one lavender with a cloak of vivid green and blue. The bottom figure, Jeremiah, also stands barefoot and holds a scroll in his right hand. His left hand is bound by a three link chain. His layered garments are elaborate and of vivid colors. A grape vine, heavy with luscious purple grapes, surrounds and ornaments the prophets.

**THE STORY:** The rose, a symbol of Mary, held by Isaiah symbolizes his prophecy: "Behold a virgin shall be with child, and bear a son, and shall call his name Immanuel." (*Isaiah 7:14*) The three link chain binding Jeremiah's left hand represents the frequent imprisonments he endured as a result of his predictions of the destruction of Jerusalem in his quest to tell of the coming of the Messiah: "Behold, the days to come, saith the Lord, that I will raise unto David a righteous Branch and a King shall reign and prosper, and shall execute judgment and justice in the earth. In his days, Judah shall be saved and Israel shall dwell safely: and this is his name whereby he shall be called, The Lord our Righteousness." (*Jeremiah 23: 5-6*)

**MEMORIAL:** Eric Gould Curry was born in Key West on August 10, 1894. His parents were Charles Jefferson Curry and Ella Isabel Gould Curry. He was first married to Viola Bauer in 1925, who died in 1929 after the birth of their son, Eric, Jr. In 1931, he married Muriel Dudderar, donor of the companion window of the prophets Daniel and Ezekiel. Eric was a CPA, with an office at 518 Fleming Street. He died in the Veteran's Hospital in Coral Gables on July 26, 1956. The window was given in his memory by his mother.

Genealogy Window/ Prophets Isaiah and Jeremiah

# Window #102
# Genealogy Window-Jesse Tree

**Phipps, Ball & Burnham**
**1920**
**13' x 5 1/2'**

*The Porter Memorial*

**DESCRIPTION:** *Jesse Tree*, the centerpiece of the magnificent lapis lazuli hued clerestory windows of the west wall, is divided into three panels and depicts the earthly family of Jesus.

At the bottom of the central panel of this intricately detailed window, Jesse is found asleep with one hand grasping a grape vine. Above him is his son, King David. The topmost figure of the central panel is the Holy Mother holding the Christ Child. The lowest figure of the right panel represents David's son, King Solomon; the middle figure is Solomon's son, King Roboam; the topmost is Abias, son of Roboam. In the left panel, the middle figure is Asa, son of Abias; the lower figure is that of Jehoshaphat, son of Asa. At the top is Joseph, the husband of Mary. The artist has included the names of all except Mary and the Christ Child, who are singularly illuminated by an aureole. A grapevine, heavily laden with grapes, encircles each person portrayed, while two red-winged angels with banderoles, hover above the scene. As the light lowers in the western sky, the window becomes an orchestration of color, glowing in shades of blue and purple.

**SYMBOLISM:** In biblical stories, the Jesse Tree represents the successive generations which culminated in Jesus. Jesse was the father of David, from whose royal lineage the Messiah was prophesized to be born: "And there shall come forth a rod out of the stem of Jesse and a Branch shall grow out of his roots." (*Isaiah 11:1*)

The metaphoric references to the grape vine found in the Bible, particularly in the Old Testament, are many. The grape vine was cultivated in the Holy Land since the earliest of times. People of the region were so dependent on its products that it became a cultural undercurrent. In the Jesse Tree window, grape vines, lush with grapes, encircle each figure, symbolizing the fruit produced by the single vine of Jesse. The Jesse Tree, representing the genealogy of Jesus, is often used during Advent as a symbolic vehicle to anticipate the arrival of Christ.

**MEMORIAL:** Among the many members of the Porter family was Dr. Joseph Y. Porter, one of the foremost experts on sanitation and hygiene in the United States and the first state health officer in Florida. He is noted for his work in controlling and preventing yellow fever, a frequent cause of death in the Florida Keys, a breeding ground for mosquitoes. He was married to Louisa Curry and their children included William Randolph Porter, married to Grace Dorgan, remembered in *Wedding Feast at Cana* (Window #109); Jennie Roberta, married to W. W. Mountjay; and Dr. J. Y. Porter, married to Beulah Brantley. Other family members are remembered in *Nativity Adoration* (Window #112).

Genealogy Window/Jesse Tree

# Window #103

# Genealogy Window-
# Prophets Daniel and Ezekiel

**Connick Associates**
**1959**
**9' 8 1/2" x 30 1/2"**

*To the Glory of God and in Memory of*
*Eric Curry    1894 - 1956    Muriel D. Curry*

**DESCRIPTION:** Two prophets, Daniel and Ezekiel, who also foretold the coming of the Messiah, are depicted in the window to the left of *Jesse Tree*. Daniel, dressed in colorful garments, carries a staff topped by a six-pointed star in his right hand; in his left hand is a scroll. Ezekiel holds a flaming torch in his right hand and a scroll in his left. Both figures stand barefoot and a grapevine heavy with fruit surrounds and ornaments them.

**SYMBOLISM:** Daniel and Ezekiel, along with Isaiah and Jeremiah in Window #101, make up the four greater prophets of the Old Testament, each of whom foretold the coming of the Messiah. The six-pointed star held by Daniel is widely regarded as a messianic symbol because of its connection with David, ancestor of the Messiah. Ezekiel's flaming torch can be interpreted as a symbol for Christ: "I am the light of the world" (*John 9:5*), or as witnessing for Christ: "Let your light so shine (*Matthew 5:16*). The grape vines, winding throughout all three genealogy windows and casting a wonderful light ranging from blue to purple, are artistic references the genealogy of Jesus from the single line of Jesse.

**MEMORIAL:** Both prophet windows were given in memory of the same person, Eric Curry, by two women central in his life. *Prophets Daniel and Ezekiel* was donated by his wife, Muriel Dudderar Curry at a cost of $1500; *Prophets Isaiah and Jeremiah* was given in his memory by his mother, Ella Isabel Gould Curry.

Both Connick Associates windows flanking the *Jesse Tree* by Phipps, Ball & Burnham, were created almost 40 years after the central window. It is remarkable that Orin Skinner from the Connick studio was able to maintain the artistic continuity of the older window.

Genealogy/Prophets Daniel and Ezekiel

# INRI, Cock and Sword of the Spirit Roundels

**Phipps, Ball & Burnham**
**1920**

*Thomas Alva Lumley*
*In Memory of My Children*
*Mary Ann Lumley   1832 - 1917*
*Thomas Lumley   1812 - 1876*

**DESCRIPTION:** Although this window located in the south tower clerestory has three numbers, in reality it is one window comprised of three panels, featuring "Signs of Our Faith" roundels. When the windows were installed they were dark, dreary, unnoticed and unappreciated for over 63 years. The artificial illumination of these windows in the spring of 1994 brought a beauty to the nave that the architect and stained glass artists must have envisioned.

**SYMBOLISM:** The right hand panel, the *INRI Roundel* (Window #104), features a roundel with a crown of thorns, a symbol for our Lord's Passion. Inside the crown of thorns are the letters "INRI," the abbreviation for the Latin, "Jesus Nazarenus Rex Judaeorum," Jesus of Nazareth, King of the Jews, representing the sign placed by Pilate on the cross above the head of Jesus at his crucifixion. (*John 19:19*) "INRI" is another representation of Jesus.

In the center panel, *Cock Roundel* (Window #105), the magnificent golden cockerel, for which this book is named, stands out against a ruby background. Representing the apostle Peter, the golden cockerel keeps a watchful eye on all those who enter St. Paul's.

The roundel of the left panel, *The Sword of the Spirit Roundel* (Window #106) contains the symbol of Saint Paul: the open Bible with the words, "Spiritus Gladius," the Sword of the Spirit. Behind the Bible is the sword of the Spirit itself. This symbol of Paul is derived from *Ephesians 6:19*: "the sword of the Spirit, which is the word of God."

**MEMORIAL:** This entire window was given by Thomas Alva Lumley, remembered in *Entry Into Jerusalem* (Window #126), in memory of his family, both deceased and living at the time of the donation. His father, Thomas Lumley, is memorialized in *INRI Roundel*. A native of Yorkshire, England, the elder Thomas Lumley, arrived in the Keys in an unusual if, not uncommon, manner. He left England as a youngster aboard a ship which wrecked on the Florida reefs and he chose to remain in Key West. He took part in the first and second Seminole Wars. He assisted in laying the cornerstone of Fort Taylor at the outbreak of the Civil War, a feat accomplished with a diving bell. He married Mary Ann Albury, who, as a child, came to Key West from the Bahamas. Their only son, Thomas Alva donated the *Cock Roundel* in her memory and gave the *Sword of the Spirit* as a remembrance to his living children: Camille, Rose, Paul, Marguerite, Flora and Loraine.

JMRJ, Cock and Sword of the Spirit Roundels

## Window #107
# Feeding the Five Thousand

**Payne Spiers Studio**
**Circa 1940   (Before 1950)**

*Presented by Marion Musgrove Closs*
*In Loving Memory of her Father*
*Joseph Charles Musgrove*
*And her Mother, Janie Cornelia Musgrove*

**DESCRIPTION:**  This narrative window is one of two from the studio of Payne Spiers; the second is *Wedding Feast at Cana* (Window #109). Each depicts a story of one of Christ's miracles as told in the New Testament Gospels.

*Feeding the Five Thousand* is divided into three panels: the central panel is devoted to Jesus and three other figures: a bearded man holding a small container of fish, a young person and an older man; the side panels are filled with a multitude of all ages. Looking down upon the scene from above the pointed Gothic canopy are two red-winged angels.

**THE STORY:**  As told in *Luke 9: 10-1*, although Jesus and his Apostles sought a quiet place of rest, many saw them going and followed.  The hour was late; the throngs hungry.  Jesus directed that they be given something to eat.  From five loaves of bread and two fishes, the host of people was fed and they were satisfied.  And those that ate numbered 5000.

**MEMORIAL:**  Joseph Musgrove is found only in the cemetery records of Key West.  The records state that he was born in the Bahamas and died when he was 40 years old on June 12, 1898.  He does not appear in the census, city directory, or in any of the records of St. Paul's, neither does Janie Cornelia Musgrove. Anything could be speculated.   It is possible that they did not live in Key West.  Perhaps he was visiting from the Bahamas, and died here suddenly, as close ties existed between Key West and Bahamian families.  It was common in those days for people to travel back and forth by boat between the islands for work, trade or for family visits.  However, St. Paul's records document the marriage of the donor, Marion Musgrove Closs, to Herbert L. Closs on January 1, 1922 by The Reverend C.R.D. Crittendon, rector of St. Paul's.  The witnesses were Captain and Mrs. Luther Pinder.

Feeding the Five Thousand

# Christ Among the Doctors

**Charles Connick Associates**

**1957**

*Samuel Mason Goldsmith & Lilla Allen Goldsmith*
*George Whiting Allen 1854 - 1922 &*
*Leonor Ximenez Allen 1855 – 1942*
*William Richard Warren & Genevieve Allen Warren*

**DESCRIPTION:** The narrative window is divided into three panels topped by two angels clad in blue hovering above the Gothic canopy. The central panel is devoted entirely to Jesus at 12 years of age. The right and left panels feature the figures of the Jewish teachers in the Temple who appear to be either directing questions or listening intently. Mary, the mother of Jesus, also appears in the left panel.

**THE STORY:** As told in *Luke 2: 42-52*, Jesus had accompanied his parents and others from Nazareth to Jerusalem for the feast of Passover. The group returned to Nazareth, but, unbeknownst to Mary and Joseph, who thought He was with other children in their group, Jesus remained in Jerusalem. After three days of searching for Him in Jerusalem, they found Him in the Temple, sitting in the midst of the doctors, or scribes, listening to them and asking questions. "And all that heard him were astonished at his understanding and answers." (*Luke: 2:47*)

**MEMORIAL:** The window is a memorial to a number of members of the same family. The central panel is in memory of George Whiting Allen, a prominent businessman and banker, and his wife Leonor Ximenez Allen.

The side panels are in memory of their two daughters, Lilla and Genevieve, and their husbands. Lilla married Samuel Mason Goldsmith, who was connected with the U.S. Weather Bureau and was an active member of St. Paul's and an ordained deacon. Genevieve married Dr. William Richard Warren who practiced medicine in Key West for many years.

Christ Among the Doctors

# Window #108

# Christic Among the Doctors

(Central Panel Detail)
**Phipps, Ball & Burnham**
1920
*In Loving Memory of*
*George Whiting Allen 1854 - 1922 &*
*Leonor Ximenez Allen 1855 – 1942*
*Samuel Mason Goldsmith & Lilla Allen Goldsmith*
*William Richard Warren & Genevieve Allen Warren*

**DESCRIPTION:** Jesus, only 12 years old, stands in the midst of the learned men in the Temple in Jerusalem as the focal point of the center panel. In this detail He is dressed in a simple square-necked tunic, sparsely decorated.

With skillful economy of brush strokes, the artist features Him as a brunette. Surrounding His head in red glass is a cross pattée, a cross of four curved arms of equal length. The right hand is raised with thumb and index finger pointing upward.

**MEMORIAL:** Of the six names of this memorial window, the story of Sam Goldsmith is told here. He came to Key West in 1920 as a meteorologist and met and married Lilla Allen. He served St. Paul's faithfully for many years as a lay reader, chimer, choir member, vestryman, and treasurer. After 40 years of dedication to the church, he became a deacon.

Sam had an outgoing personality and a ready wit. The Reverend James MacConnell, former rector, in his letter to Rex Weech dated October 15, 1971, recalls two tales of old Key West in which Samuel Goldsmith is the main character. They both involve a visit to the island by Bishop Wing.

In the first story, Samuel Goldsmith met Bishop Wing with a car whose license plate was about five years old. When the Bishop commented, Sam explained. "We in Key West get a license when we buy the car and don't bother about any after that like they do on the mainland because we can't go anywhere but on the island."

In the second, Sam and the Bishop were walking down Duval Street when a man asked them if they wanted a drink. The Bishop asked if Sam knew anything about Prohibition and if they had any law enforcement officers on the island. Sam explained patiently that it was the Sheriff who offered then the drink!

## Christ Among the Doctors

(Central Panel Detail)

# Christ Among the Doctors

(Right Panel Detail)
Phipps, Ball & Burnham
1920

*In Loving Memory of*
*George Whiting Allen 1854 - 1922 &*
*Leonor Ximenez Allen 1855 – 1942*
*Samuel Mason Goldsmith & Lilla Allen Goldsmith*
*William Richard Warren & Genevieve Allen Warren*

**DESCRIPTION:** Through the detailed facial expressions and the hand gestures, the artist conveys the attentiveness of the elders of the Temple as they listen to the young Jesus. The richness of their dress symbolizes their stature and stands out in contrast to the simplicity of the youth's white robes.

**MEMORIAL:** Since the window is in memory of an entire family, it is fitting that the story of the wedding of Genevieve and Richard is recounted to provide a glimpse into life in Key West in the early 20th century.

It was January 21, 1911. St. Paul's third church had been destroyed in the hurricane of 1909. Genevieve Allen and Dr. William R. Warren would be married in an Episcopal ceremony at the nearby Old Stone Methodist Church, with The Reverend C. T. Stout, rector of St. Paul's officiating.

The church was crowded inside and out for this was a brilliant social event. When the strains of the wedding march burst forth, all eyes turned towards the door. After the bridesmaids came the maid of honor, Lilla Allen, sister of the bride, wearing pink marquisette over blue satin, trimmed in pink marabou and lace. Her headdress was pink tulle and blue marabou. She carried a bouquet of La France roses. Then the bride entered. Escorted by her father, Hon. George W. Allen, she wore a satin wedding gown with a crystal bodice trimmed with handsome pearls and heirloom lace. Her long tulle veil was caught up with orange blossoms bodice and she carried a shower bouquet of bride's roses and lilies of the valley.

Waiting at the altar was the groom, Dr. William R. Warren. The wedding was performed under a large white wedding bell, suspended by a triangle trimmed with greens and pink roses. The triangle and the bell were illuminated by many miniature pink and blue electric lights. The mother of the bride, Leonor Ximenez Allen wore a stunning gown of black spangled beaded net over white satin.

One of the important moments of the event was the cutting of the heart-shaped wedding cake at the reception. The custom at the time was to place various articles in the cake batter before baking: a ring to signify an early wedding; a dime, a forerunner of wealth; a thimble, a hint to sew a wedding dress; and a pair of mittens.

# Christ Among the Doctors
### (Right Panel Detail)

# Wedding Feast at Cana

**Payne Spiers Studio**
**1930 or 1940**

*To The Glory of God*
*And In Loving Memory of*
*Grace Dorgan Porter*

**DESCRIPTION:** The lovely narrative window is the second by the Payne Spiers Studio in St. Paul's Church and, as does its companion, *Feeding the Five Thousand* (Window #107), tells the story of one of Christ's miracles. Although the stories are different, there are some striking artistic similarities between the two windows.

The two red-winged angels hovering above the Gothic canopy and the detailed work just beneath the pointed canopy are similar, as is the bottom border of each panel. The rendering of the clouds in both windows are also similar, as is the gentleness of the facial expressions.

The central panel of *Wedding Feast at Cana* is devoted to Jesus and his mother, Mary. In the right panel, two people are taking part in the festivities of the wedding; a third tastes the wine. In the left panel, two servants are engaged in pouring water into a large container. The detailed rendering of the color gradations of the wine pouring from the jug tell the story of the miracle.

**THE STORY:** Considered to be the first of Jesus' public miracles, the events of a marriage in Cana described in *John 2:1-11*, are beautifully and simply expressed in this window. Jesus, his mother, Mary, and His disciples were invited to a wedding in Cana. At a certain point, Mary noticed the wine had run out and expressed this to Jesus. He directed the servants to fill six stone water pots with water and take them to the steward. When the steward tasted the water, he found it to be wine. This event is said to have contributed to the awakening of His disciples who witnessed the event: "This beginning of miracles did Jesus in Cana of Galilee, and manifested forth his glory; and his disciples believed on him." (*John 2:11*)

**MEMORIAL:** Grace Dorgan was born November 3, 1876 in Mobile, Alabama. Her parents, Mr. and Mr. Lyman C. Dorgan, were one of the best known families in Alabama. Grace married William R. Porter in the Presbyterian Church in Mobile on January 19, 1891. They made their home in Key West, where Grace took an active interest in the affairs of the First Presbyterian Church, the Woman's Club and the Key West Garden Club. Grace died on March 24, 1930. William R. Porter was president of the First National Bank of Key West and for many years was a member of the Monroe County Commission. Other members of the Porter family are remembered in *Jesse Tree* (Window #102) and *Nativity Adoration* (Window #112).

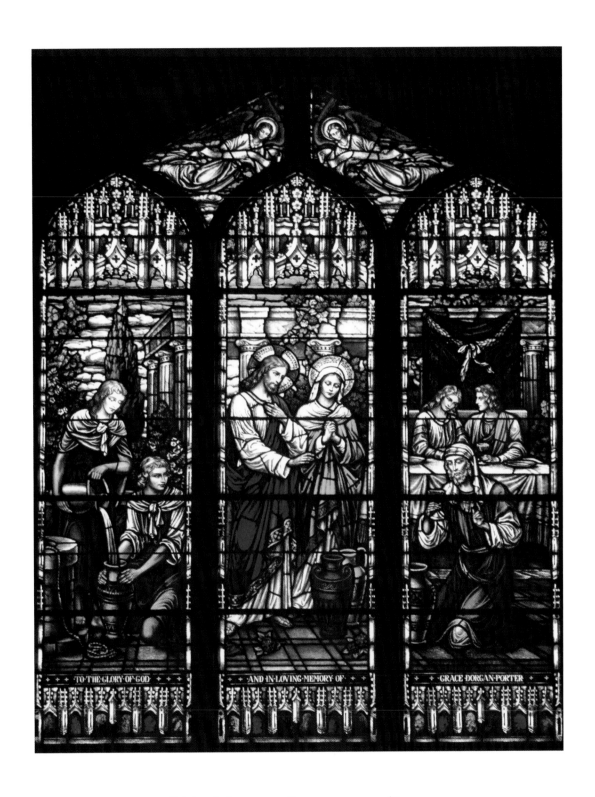

Wedding Feast at Cana

# Window #109
# Wedding Feast at Cana

**(Left Panel Detail)**
**Payne Spiers Studio**
**1930 or 1940**

*To The Glory of God*
*And In Loving Memory of*
*Grace Dorgan Porter*

**DESCRIPTION:** In the left panel of *Wedding Feast at Cana* there are two servants beside a well, one standing and one kneeling. In the background are a cypress tree, clouds and an abundance of flowers.

**SYMBOLISM:** In this panel, the servants have drawn water from the well, as instructed by Jesus, and are engaged in pouring it from one container to the other. The artist has chosen this moment to depict the miracle of water turning into wine. This act has been accomplished artistically by the gradual change in the color of the liquid as it pours from the jug. The liquid begins as white and gradually deepens to a deep rose as it enters the second jug.

**A STORY OF FAITH:** Terry Waite, the Anglican who was kidnapped by Shiite fundamentalists in Beirut in 1987 and released in November 1991, believes his faith was the foundation of his survival. He found solace in the story about how Christ changed water into wine. Waite recounted that a conversion of circumstances has to take place deep within yourself: "Like water into wine, the most miserable surroundings can be transformed – if you allow the transformation process to take place inside you. Although that's not easy, it is possible. Slowly, Slowly."

Wedding Feast at Cana
(Left Panel Detail)

# Window #110
# Christ with the Elders-Road to Emmaus

**Harry Taylor**
**Mid 1970s (perhaps 1977)**

*In Loving Memory of*
*Milton E. Sawyer and Le Roy Voght*
*From a Devoted Wife*
*Ruth G. Sawyer*

**DESCRIPTION:** There are many similarities between this window and *Christ the Fisherman* (Window #124), both by local stained glass artist, Harry Taylor. These windows are more contemporary in style than the older windows in the church. Placed as companion clerestory windows on the west wall of the south and north transepts, the figures are set in a landscape background essential to the narrative. Both emit a warm golden light, sparked by vivid red and green, in contrast with the predominantly cooler tones found in many of the older windows. The top and bottom portion of both windows, as well as the borders, are identical. The placement and position of Christ are similar, as are the expressions on the faces of the men pictured in each window. The two stories they depict, however, are clearly told in the details that make them different.

*Christ with the Elders-Road to Emmaus* shows two men walking with Christ along a road of stone leading from a city, engaged in conversation. Christ's bright red robe stands out in vivid contrast to the surrounding golden hues. When the window was first installed, the nail marks in the hands and feet of Jesus were omitted. Father Potter, the rector, requested this detail be added. These are an important detail as the story takes place after Christ's Crucifixion and Resurrection.

**THE STORY:** As told in *Luke 24: 13-31*, shortly after the Crucifixion and the Resurrection, two of Jesus' disciples were going to the village of Emmaus, a few miles from Jerusalem, discussing the all the strange events of the day. While they were walking and talking together, Jesus drew near and walked along with them. Jesus spoke to them, inquiring about the nature of their conversation and the reason for their sadness, but they did not recognize Him. It was only later, when they stopped in Emmaus and He took the bread, blessed and broke it, did they realize the identity of their traveling companion: "And their eyes were opened, and they knew him; and he vanished from sight." (*Luke 24:31*)

**MEMORIAL:** Ruth Gandolph, the donor of the window, was first married to Le Roy Voght, a barber. Sometime after his death she married Milton E. Sawyer, a widower. Milton was Assistant Postmaster and a devoted churchman, serving on the vestry of St. Paul's. By his former marriage he had two sons, Eugene and Jackson.

Ruth Sawyer chose the theme of this narrative window because Milton, her second husband, often spoke of Christ appearing to two wayfarers. For a time this window was called Wayfarers Window.

Christ with the Elders/The Road to Emmaus

# Window #111
# Saint Luke

**Studio Unknown**
**After 1927; before 1950**

*St. Luke The Beloved Physician*
*Joseph Yates Porter*
*October 21, 1847 – March 10, 1927*

**DESCRIPTION:** St. Paul's has four windows representing the Gospels, accounts of the life and work of Christ, gracing the church. All are smaller clerestory windows located in the transept of the church. *Saint Luke* (Window #111) and *Saint John* (Window #113) are in the south transept; *Saint Matthew* and *Saint Mark* are in the north transept. With the exception of *Saint John*, which was designed by Phipps, Ball & Burnham, the artists are unknown.

Window #111, a small figural clerestory window in the south transept, is of Saint Luke, pictured as a bearded old man. In his left hand is a feathered quill. Luke is wearing loose-fitting garments of varied colors: blue, green, red and gold. The slippers on his feet are rose-colored. Above his head is a banderole which reads: St. Luke The Beloved Physician. The usual spelling of Luke is assumed to be abbreviated as the "e" cannot be seen. It is interesting to note the unknown artist of this window has conformed to the style of its companion window, *Saint John* (Window #113), installed earlier by Phipps, Ball & Burnham, on the opposite side of the *Nativity Adoration* (Window #112).

**SAINT LUKE:** Luke was a native of Antioch, a man of culture, a physician, and reputed to be an artist. His stories of Christ's life are swift moving, in detailed chronological order, and stress Christ's humanity and concern about the welfare of all people.

**MEMORIAL:** It is undoubtedly by design that this window featuring "Luke the beloved physician" (*Colossians 4:14*) was given in memory of Joseph Yates Porter, also a physician, noted for his efforts to quell dreaded epidemics of yellow fever. He was born in Key West on October 21, 1847, to Mary Randolph Porter, two weeks after the death of his father J. Y. Porter. He attended public schools in Burlington, New Jersey and graduated from Jefferson Medical College of Philadelphia in 1870. After entering the U.S. Army, he was sent to Fort Jefferson, a Civil War fort located on a small island 70 miles west of Key West, where he spent three and a half years. When Florida organized the State Board of Health in 1889, he was the first state health officer and continued in that capacity for many years. On June 1, 1870, he married Louise Curry of Key West. They were the parents of four children: William Randolph, Mary Louise, Jennie Roberta, and Dr. Joseph Yates Porter, Jr.

Saint Luke

# Window #112
# Nativity Adoration

**Phipps, Ball & Burnham**
**1920**

*In Loving Memory of my Grandfather Thomas Mann Randolph*
*In Loving Memory of my Mother Mary Randolph Porter*
*And Grandmother Susan Eaton Randolph*
*In Loving Memory of my Father Joseph Yates Porter*

**DESCRIPTION:** This magnificent clerestory window in the south transept contains three panels depicting a favorite subject of ecclesiastical art: the birth of Jesus. The center panel of the traditional nativity scene is devoted to the Holy Family; the right depicts the shepherds; the left, the three kings. Above the silver stain canopy are two angels with banderoles proclaiming: Alleluiah, Alleluiah, Alleluiah.

In the center panel, Joseph stands behind Mary, who is pictured in an awkward stance. The proportions of the Christ Child are not that of a newborn baby, and the lamb in the foreground appears stiff and wooden. Despite these issues with artistic perspective, especially outstanding in the painting is the treatment of the draping of all the garments. One can almost feel the texture of the fabrics. Noteworthy is the apparent softness of the ermine mantle of one king. The kings wear no crowns, but upon close observance, one crown can be seen carefully laid upon the ground, a gesture representing the removal of royal headgear in honor of the King of Kings.

**MEMORIAL:** The donor of this window is Dr. Joseph Yates Porter, Sr., who is remembered in the preceding window, *Saint Luke* (Window #111). When Dr. Porter's grandfather, Thomas Mann Randolph, was captain of the United States revenue cutter *Washington*, he met and married Susan Browne. They were the parents of William B, and Mary Ann.

A beautiful and accomplished person, Mary Ann was the first organist of St. Paul's. She married Joseph Yates Porter of South Carolina, who died two weeks before Mary Ann gave birth to their only child. Mary Ann died at an early age of yellow fever, leaving behind young Joseph Yates Porter who grew up to become a doctor, famous for his efforts to control and prevent the disease that took his mother.

Nativity Adoration

# Window #113
# Saint John

**Phipps, Ball & Burnham (conjecture)**
**1920**

*"Thy Word is a Lamp Unto My Feet and a Light Unto My Path."*
*In Memoriam Gilbert Higgs D.D.*

**DESCRIPTION:** This small figural clerestory window in the south transept depicts Saint John. He is featured as a young, clean-shaven man wearing a loose-fitting white garment and a red cloak. Above his head is a banderole with the words, "Thy Word is a Lamp Unto My Feet and a Light Unto My Path." (*Psalm 119: 105*). He holds an open book in his left hand and a quill in his right.

**SAINT JOHN:** The fourth Gospel in the New Testament is attributed to John, son of Zebedee, although, as with the other Gospels, the author is not named. Written perhaps 60 or more years after the Crucifixion, his Gospel brings out the spiritual significance behind Jesus' works and words. From John comes one of the most often quoted of all Bible verses: "For God so loved the world that he gave his only begotten Son, that whoever believeth in him shall not perish but have everlasting life." (*John 3:16*)

**MEMORIAL:** Gilbert Higgs was born in Bermuda in June 1844. He became rector of St. Paul's in 1890. It was here he met Clara Victoria Hertell of Key West and they were married in a lovely ceremony with Bishop William Crane Gray officiating. Their two daughters, Ruth and Marian, were the first children born in the rectory.

Dr. Higgs was a man of great energy and fine artistic taste. He planned a Victorian garden on the church grounds that became one of the showplaces of the city. The roses grown there were sold by a young man, Eugene Lowe, the proceeds of which were used to buy a processional cross. Dr. Higgs instituted the first vested choir, began the use of candles on the altar, and ensured that the wall in front of the church was completed in time for his wedding on May 9, 1894. In that year he served as Archdeacon of Monroe, Lee and Dade counties. He covered this expansive territory at a time when travel from the Keys to the mainland could be accomplished only by boat.

When services in the home of Clement Knowles, Sr. resulted in the formation of (First) Holy Innocents Mission, opposite the fire station on Grinnell Street, Dr. Higgs designed and built the altar. When the mission closed its doors in 1917, the altar was moved to St. Paul's Lady Chapel in the south transept, where it was used for many years.

Dr. and Mrs. J. Y. Porter, Sr. were the donors of the window. All three clerestory windows in the south transept, which in unison bathe the Lady Chapel in magnificent light, were donated by the Porter family.

Saint John

# Window #114

# Saint Barnabas

**Powell Brothers & Sons**

**2003**

*"In Thanksgiving for the Founders of St. Paul's Memorial Foundation"*

**DESCRIPTION:** The most recent additions to the glorious windows of St. Paul's are four windows in the chancel designed by Powell Brothers & Sons. All four are illuminated artificially from behind as these windows have no source of natural light. The choir room is located behind the windows on the right; the sacristy is behind the windows on the left.

In an effort to integrate the newer windows into the feeling of the older ones, these four windows are painted, stained, etched and leaded, using techniques virtually unchanged since the 13th century. Gothic elements such as the pointed arch are artfully combined with a more contemporary background of rectangular glass and simple imagery. The focal point becomes the central, solitary figure.

In this window, just over the door leading to the choir room, Saint Barnabas is pictured in a deep purple robe on an equally deep and serene rich red and deep blue background.

**THE STORY:** Saint Barnabas was one of the earliest Christian disciples, preaching to both Gentiles and Jews. His close association with Saint Paul, patron saint of St. Paul's Church, made him a natural choice to represent the work of those honored in the window: the Founders of St. Paul's Memorial Foundation, the selfless sponsors of the church. It was Barnabas who sponsored Paul in front of the skeptics who remembered Paul's former fierce ways. Together they traveled throughout distant regions on a journey of conversion, enduring opposition and persecution.

**MEMORIAL:** St. Paul's Memorial Foundation was established in 1987 by five parishioners in an effort to save the church which had deteriorated considerably over the years. These founding five were Harry Knight, Anne McKee, Sebastian Cabrera, Leon Sands and Hugh Papy. Raising the enormous sums needed for the daunting task required a multifaceted approach, and this group left no stone unturned. According to Harry Knight, the Foundation's first president and long standing secretary, from the pulpit they asked parishioners for funds; they privately talked to people in the community; through State Representative Ron Saunders, they appealed to the state of Florida and received matching funds; they created projects where everyone could participate with whatever means they could.

The result of this local effort was two-fold: the church was gradually repaired and by involving everyone, a sense of unity among all participants, both full-time and winter residents, was created. A collective sense of local pride developed while a solid financial reserve to care for the historic church was built through on-going contributions. In the words of Harry Knight, "We can now rest in peace."

IN THANKSGIVING FOR
THE FOUNDERS
OF ST. PAUL'S
MEMORIAL FOUNDATION

Saint Barnabas

# Window #115
# Deborah and a Scroll Under the Palms

**Powell Brothers & Sons**
**1999**

*In Loving Memory of Paulie T. Raymond*
*From Bob and Louise Taylor*

**DESCRIPTION:** Deborah sits reflectively considering a scroll, symbolic of her role as judge and community leader. The smaller medallion above Deborah contains two crossed palms, Christian symbols for victory and rejoicing and, in a secular sense also represent Key West. As with the other three Powell windows inside the chancel, the handmade, imported glass contributes to this rich and vibrant window.

**THE STORY:** The story of Deborah is told twice: in *Judges 4*, in prose; in *Judges 5*, in poetry. From the latter comes *The Song of Deborah*, one of the most literary pieces in the Bible. Deborah was a poet and a judge of Israel, the only woman to hold that office. Under her guidance, Barak conquered Sisera and delivered Israel from the oppression of the Canaanite King Jabin. As depicted in the window in St. Paul's, "she dwelt under the palm tree of Deborah between Ramah and Bethel in mount Ephraim: and the children of Israel came up to her for judgment." *(Judges 4:5)*

**MEMORIAL:** Paulette (Paulie) Claire Taylor Raymond (1949-1994) was born in Wakefield, Rhode Island, the middle daughter of Louise and Bob Taylor. She received a degree in Journalism from Michigan State University. She married Ray Raymond and they had one daughter, Colleen Louisa. Paulie was a columnist and Lifestyle section editor for the *Key West Citizen*, demonstrating a talent for discovering unusual facts about extraordinary and ordinary folks. Paulie charitably assisted Literacy Volunteers, Helpline, The Salvation Army's board and KWAMI.

The donors, Louise and Bob Taylor, felt that in her brief life their daughter Paulie's literary and charitable contributions exemplified Deborah's life of justice and scholarship. *Zacchaeus Climbing the Sycamore Tree* (Window #119), on the north wall of the chancel directly opposite Deborah, was given in memory of Bob Taylor, Paulie's father. The loving thread between the two is Louise Stroune McClanahan Taylor, mother to one, wife to the other.

Deborah and a Scroll Under the Palms

# Saint Paul on Mars Hill

**Phipps, Ball & Burnham**
**1920**

**In Memory of Bertha Curry Bott**
**1888 – 1919**

**DESCRIPTION:** One of two windows featuring Saint Paul, the patron saint of St. Paul's Church, which appropriately flank the centerpiece of the church, *Crucifixion*, the great east window behind the High Altar.

The narrative window portrays Saint Paul preaching in Athens on Mars Hill. The bearded Paul is simply dressed in a light colored garment with a ruby cloak draped over his body. His right hand is extended upward and in the background is a Greek temple. Just below the ornate silver stain canopy, are the words: "Whom Therefore ye Ignorantly Worship." Three people are listening intently to Paul, two of whom are women. Of note in all the narrative windows by Phipps, Ball & Burnham are the size and gaze of the eyes of all the figures portrayed.

**THE STORY:** *St. Paul on Mars Hill* depicts Saint Paul during the course of his ministry, whereas the companion window, *Saint Paul on the Damascus Road* depicts Paul as Saul in his pre-Christian days. Once again, the placement of these windows is thoughtful as it was only following the Crucifixion and Resurrection that Paul converted to Christianity.

During the course of his ministry, Paul traveled thousands of miles by sea and land, establishing many congregations in Europe and Asia Minor. The Greek Temple in the background, symbolizing Athens, is a reference to his travels. As a result of his conversion to Christianity, he endured much: imprisonment, stoning, beatings and being shipwrecked. On his journeys he encountered dangers around every turn: in rivers, in the desert, in the cities and from highwaymen along the roads, none of which deterred him on his mission.

**MEMORIAL:** This window is in memory of Bertha Curry Bott, who was born in 1888 and died in 1919. She married Shirley Cristie Bott on January 19, 1904, with The Reverend William Curtis White, priest in charge of the (First) Holy Innocence Mission, performing the ceremony. Their daughter, Euphemia (Mary E.) was born on April 5, 1905. The 1920 census, taken after the death of Bertha, documents that Shirley Bott was a real estate salesman living at 229 Caroline Street with his daughter, Euphemia, 15 at that time.

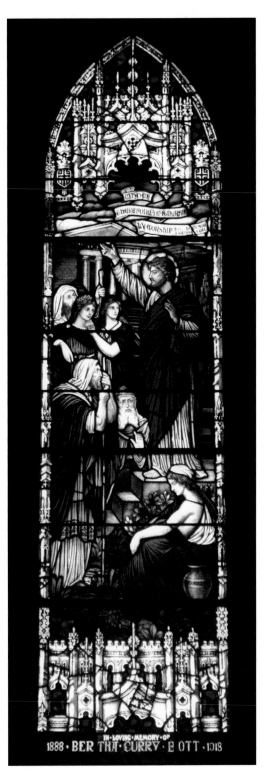

Saint Paul on Mars Hill

# Window #117
# Crucifixion

## (Right Panel Detail)
## Phipps, Ball & Burnham
## 1920

### *St. Paul's Church Sunday School*

**DESCRIPTION:** The narrative theme of the entire glorious and ornate three-paneled window is the Crucifixion. The narrative is divided into three panels, linked together via the ornate silver stain canopy under each of the three gothic arches.

The right panel depicts three figures: a bearded older man, Saint John, and a Roman centurion. In this detail, the handsome Roman soldier, holding a spear, is in full military dress. Centurions were in command of 100 soldiers, drilling them and inspecting their arms, supplies and food. They also supervised the scourging and capital punishment. The centurion represented here stands out, for around his waist he wears a belt with a red jewel buckle which draws the eye.

**THE STORY:** John is the only disciple recorded to have been present at the crucifixion of Christ, and he is depicted in the *Crucifixion*. When Jesus looked down from the cross and "therefore saw his mother and the disciple stranding by, whom he loved, he saith unto his mother, Woman, behold thy son! Then saith he to the disciple, Behold thy mother! And from that hour that disciple took her unto his own home." (*John 19:26-27*)

The centurion in this detail is the army officer in charge of the four soldiers who put Jesus to death. Despite his role, he is honored in this depiction of the Crucifixion for the realization that came upon him at the time of Jesus' death. As recorded in *Luke 23: 46-47*: "And when Jesus had cried out with a loud voice, he said, Father, into thy hands I commend my spirit: and having said thus, he gave up the ghost. Now when the centurion saw what was done, he glorified God saying, Certainly this was a righteous man."

**MEMORIAL:** Among the senior members of St. Paul's there are a few who remember the nickels and dimes they gave towards the building of the fourth church, but none remember the details of this window specifically. The Minutes of the Vestry, dated July 19, 1919, recorded that Mr. W. G. Ball submitted a proposition to furnish a number of cathedral glass windows. At that meeting, the vestry signed an agreement for placing a Sunday School window in the chancel.

Since this detail portrays an army officer, it is fitting to remember The Reverend Osgood Herrick who, for a time during the Civil War, was both rector of St. Paul's and chaplain of the U. S. Army in Key West and Fort Jefferson. During the yellow fever epidemic, he ministered to the sick and dying of the community and the military and was made chaplain of the post. Later during his career he served as Army chaplain at the Chapel of the Centurion in Fort Monroe, Virginia.

# Crucifixion
### (Right Panel Detail)

# Crucifixion

**(Center Panel Detail)**
**Phipps, Ball & Burnham**
**1920**

*In Loving Memory of Mary Elizabeth Lowe*
*Born 1837   Died 1919   and*
*John Lowe Jr.*
*Born 1833   Died 1917*

**DESCRIPTION AND SYMBOLISM:** The center panel of the *Crucifixion*, the spiritual and inspiring focal point of the church, depicts the crucifixion of Jesus. It is intricately detailed and filled with symbolism.  Near the top of the cross appears a sign bearing the inscription, INRI, letters which stand for the phrase in Latin which translates to: "Jesus of Nazareth, King of the Jews."  Placed on the cross in mockery by Pilate, it is regarded as a symbol of faith. Surrounding the entire figure of our Savior is an irradiance of light, an aureole, interspersed with six doves, representing the Holy Spirit. The oblong aureole surrounding the crucified Jesus is said to represent His ascension into heaven and the Glory of God.  Against a ruby background, the word, "Sanctus", Latin for holy, is on either side of the body of Jesus. In the background are the sun, the moon and four stars depicting the passage of time during the Crucifixion; the moon and the stars tell of the ninth hour, the time of Jesus' death. The jar on the ground symbolizes anointment, the sacred rite of consecration; the lily foretells the Resurrection.

**MEMORIAL:** John Lowe, Jr., son of John Lowe, Sr. and Bianca Kemp Lowe, was born on March 11, 1833 on Green Turtle Cay, Bahamas.  He married Mary Elizabeth on December 15, 1856 in a ceremony performed by The Reverend Osgood Herrick, rector of St. Paul's. They lived in a lovely, spacious home at 620 Southard Street with their children Edward, Eugene, George, Stephen, Charles and Emma.

John Jr., largely self-educated, began work at the age of 12 in his brother-in-law's firm, Browne and Curry.  He became a pioneer in the maritime industry contributing to Key West's status in the mid-1880s as the richest city in Florida, attributable to the lucrative wrecking, or salvaging, industry.  He was in the mercantile business and in the sponge industry, owning 15 to 20 schooners engaged in both sponging and wrecking.  His wharf became the largest sponge market in the world; his shipping enterprise supplied Key West with building materials, live beef cattle, vegetables, tropical fruit from South and Central America, and many other necessities.

John Lowe, Jr. faithfully served St. Paul's in many ways.  He was a vestryman during the building of the fourth and present church, but died before its completion.

# Crucifixion
## (Center Panel Detail)

# Window #117
# Crucifixion

**(Left Panel Detail)**
**Phipps, Ball & Burnham**
**1920**

*Leonora J. Seymour, Hiram A. Seymour*
*Charles E. Seymour, John C. Seymour*

**DESCRIPTION:** Completing the narrative, the left panel of the *Crucifixion* depicts some of those who observed the death of Christ. In this detail of the left panel there are three people: a bearded man and two women. Their garments are elaborate and fall in soft folds.

**THE STORY:** A great number of people witnessed the crucifixion. Among them were Jesus' mother, Mary, and Mary Magdalene, represented by the two women in this detail.

**MEMORIAL:** Hiram Seymour was born in the Bahamas in 1849. His father was born in England; his mother in Bermuda. He came to the United States in 1868, settling in Key West as the owner of a grocery store and sea captain.

Leonora Jane Dunn was born in Florida in 1855. Her father was from Ireland; her mother from Florida. Hiram and Leonora were married on March 7, 1872, with The Reverend William T. Saunders, rector of St. Paul's officiating.

Hiram and Leonora were the parents of a number of children: Hiram, Charles, John, Mary Nellie, and Jennie. Baby Hiram died the day he was born, having lived long enough to be baptized. Charles was born on March 11, 1876, became a steam engineer and was married to Emma Risch on November 18, 1909, in a service conducted by The Reverend Charles Stout, rector of St. Paul's. *The Transfiguration* (Window #127) is in memory of Jennie and Nellie. Little is known of John other than his birth on February 1, 1883 and his death at the age of 30 on July 3, 1917.

Since the window was installed in 1920, it is presumed that Captain Hiram Seymour, who died in 1922 at the age of 73, was the donor of this portion of the *Crucifixion*.

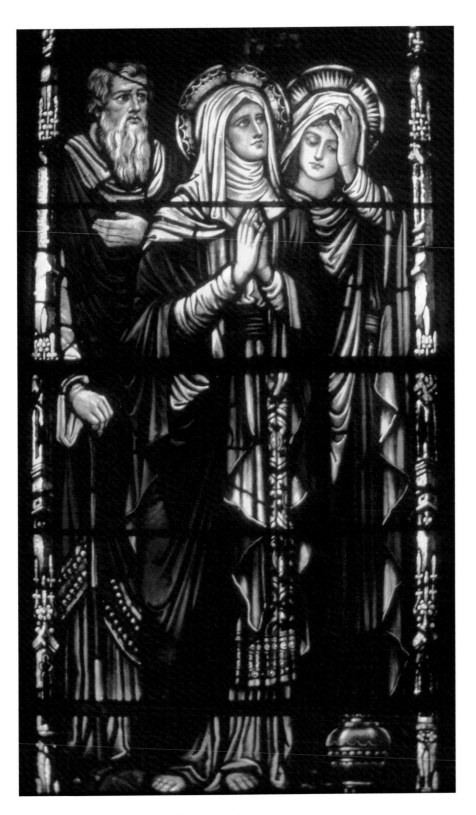

# Crucifixion
**(Left Panel Detail)**

# Window #118
# Saint Paul on the Damascus Road

**Phipps, Ball & Burnham**
**1920**

*George Dean Warren   Born Oct. 21, 1837   Died Sept. 16, 1914*
*Susan Mary Warren   Aug. 21, 1842*

**DESCRIPTION:**  The second narrative window featuring Saint Paul, the patron saint of the church, depicts a group of people on their journey to Damascus.  Among them is Paul before his conversion to Christianity.  Paul, then called Saul, is pictured lying on the ground, appearing to be looking towards the rays of light coming from the top center of the window.

**THE STORY:**  The window tells the story of the incident that led to Paul's conversion.  Prior to his conversion, Paul was bent on vicious persecution against Christ's followers, for whom he had written permission from the high priests to bring in bonds to Jerusalem.  As told in *Acts 9*, while traveling to Damascus on this mission, a bright light came down from heaven and Paul fell.  As he fell, he heard a voice. Paul "trembling and astonished said, Lord, what wilt though thou have me do? And the Lord said unto him, Arise, and go into the city, and it shall be told thee what thou must do." (*Acts 9:6*)  Paul, blinded for three days from this experience, was led into Damascus, where he regained his sight, was baptized, and began his journey of preaching that Christ was the Son of God.

Both patron saint windows were designed by the architect to ventilate the sanctuary by a pulley system of ropes or chains operated from the floor.  In this manner the bottom section of the windows opened out to let in the breeze.  With the advent of air-conditioning the windows were stabilized.  During that process, which involved removing the windows, sections were reversed, resulting in one of Paul's shoes from the Road to Damascus appearing in Mars Hill window.  This gave rise to a subtle joke:  "Did you know that Paul lost his shoe on the road to Damascus and it was found on Mars Hill?"  The sections were repositioned, and today Paul's shoe is on the "right" foot!

**MEMORIAL:**  The window is in memory of George Dean Warren and his wife, Susan Mary.  George was born in Pawtucket, Rhode Island, and reared in Providence.  He came to Key West during the Civil War as a carpenter, applying his skills to the construction of Fort Taylor.  He remained in Key West and entered the hardware business where he stayed until his retirement.  Susan Mary, daughter of William and Sarah Johnson, was born in the Bahamas and came to Key West with her parents.  She and George were married on May 5, 1862, with The Reverend Robert J. McCook performing the ceremony.  By 1880 they were the parents of a number of children ranging in age from 17 to five months: John, George, Charlotte, Thomas, Mary, William and Susan.  William practiced medicine in Key West for many years.  He and his wife, Genevieve, are remembered in *Wedding Feast at Cana* (Window #108).

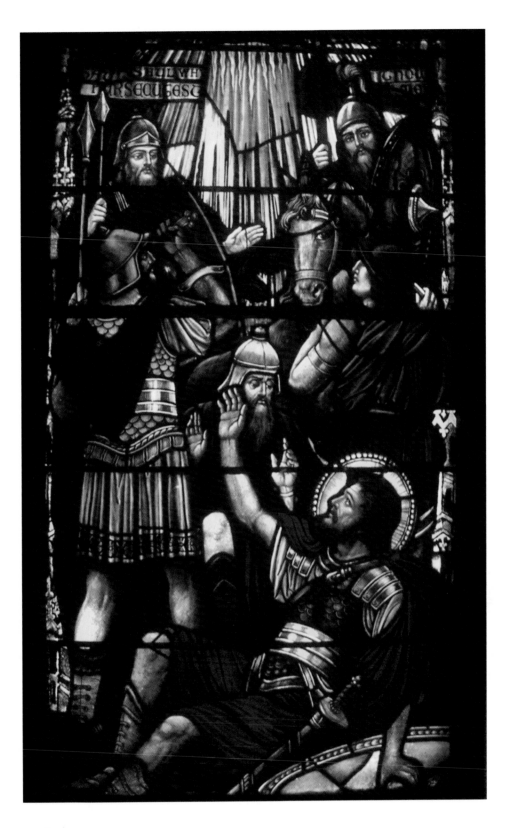

Saint Paul on the Road to Damascus

# Window #119
# Zacchaeus Climbing the Sycamore Tree

**Powell Brothers & Sons**
**1999**

*In Loving Memory of Bob Taylor*
*From Louise M. Taylor*

**DESCRIPTION:** The window is designed in the same manner as the other three Powell windows in the chancel. It is neo-Gothic in design, with a pictorial central medallion set in rectangles of rich and deeply colored glass. The larger central medallion depicts Zacchaeus in the sycamore tree. In the smaller medallion at the top of the window, there are two representations of Christ: two fish and the Greek letters IOXYC.

**THE STORY:** Being small of stature, Zacchaeus, the tax collector, climbed a tree to obtain a better view of Jesus as he entered Jerusalem. He not only caught a glimpse, but "When Jesus came to that place, he looked up and saw him and said to him, Zacchaeus, make haste and come down, for today I must abide at thy house." (*Luke 19:5*)

**MEMORIAL:** Robert Douglas Taylor was born in Providence, Rhode Island to Evelyn Groby and Lyman Taylor in 1917. He attended Rhode Island State University, studying engineering through the GI Bill. After graduation he moved to Key West with his wife, Louise, and their three young daughters to begin a 30 year career with the Federal Aviation Agency.

Bob faithfully, quietly and humorously served St. Paul's as a vestryman, usher, property handyman and installer of storm windows. Louise said that the Zacchaeus story reminded her of Bob because he was shy and performed tasks in a roundabout way. His enthusiasm for St. Paul's was second only to his enthusiasm for sports. In addition to fishing, a secondary theme in the smaller medallion, he played golf and tennis religiously. If you look closely, you may be able to find the tiny golf club and tennis racket cleverly worked into the foliage of the sycamore tree!

The donor, Louise Stoune McClanahan Taylor (1919-1998) was born to Julia Downing and Cleveland McClanahan on a farm in Chocolocco, Alabama. She received a master's degree in mathematics and physics from the University of Alabama which she utilized during her 30-year career as Navy mathematician and director of Naval Ordinance Unit. She was proud of her Honorary Conch appointment by Wilhelmina Harvey, Key West's first woman mayor. During her 45 years of service as trustee, treasurer and vestryman, Louise was St. Paul's watchdog. As an active member of Episcopal Church Women, she made countless egg and tuna sandwiches for the homeless. As a modest and humble person, a devoted attendee of Morning Prayer and a frequent lay reader, we fondly recall her broad smile and her soft Alabama accent. She was a staunch and true friend to many, and was also the donor, along with her husband, of *Deborah and a Scroll under the Palms* (Window # 115) on the opposing chancel wall.

Zachaeus Climbing the Sycamore Tree

# Window #120

# Miriam

**Powell Brothers & Sons**
**2003**

*To the Glory of God*
*For Blessings Received By*
*Anne and Ross McKee*

**DESCRIPTION:** The fourth window in the church by Powell Brothers adds balanced rich light to the chancel. It features Miriam the Prophetess of the Old Testament playing a tambourine against a dark red background. As in the other Powell windows, the border is interspersed with the five-pointed Epiphany Star.

**THE STORY:** The selection of Miriam, the prophetess of the Old Testament who led the women in song, as the subject for the window in this location is a nice one. From her location over the door leading to the sacristy, Miriam looks down on the choir of St. Paul's as they lead the congregation in song: "Sing ye to the Lord, for he hath triumphed gloriously." (*Exodus 15:21*)

**MEMORIAL:** Anne and Ross McKee, originally from Newfoundland, have been faithful servants of Saint Paul's. Great humanitarians and philanthropists, their involvement in the successful completion of numerous projects in St. Paul's and their support of the visual and performing arts in Key West through generous grants to local artists have been their enduring gift to the community and the church.

Active generous, intelligent, warm and humorously spirited into his nineties, Ross died on August 19, 2006. According to Father David Wilt, while never admitting he belonged to any church, Ross nonetheless loved to talk about religion. His intelligence and gentleness will long be remembered.

According to all who know Anne, along with her many other interests she has been a driving force in Saint Paul's. As one of the five founding members of St. Paul's Memorial Foundation, which like the phoenix rising from the ashes helped bring a crumbling church back to its former glory, Anne has been instrumental in getting projects wished for completed.

One example of her determined and giving spirit says fellow Memorial Foundation founding member, Harry Knight, was the day she stood up in church and challenged the congregation to match her $8000 gift for the re-leading of one of the great clerestory windows. Among her many projects, Anne initiated and continues to spearhead the annual Christmas program raising funds for the organ renovation, and also coordinates the annual fundraising fashion show.

When Anne is in town, each Sunday at the 9 o'clock service Father David Wilt, rector of St. Paul's, looks for her, clearly recognizable in her red hat. Father Wilt notes that although she enjoys this particular service because it includes wonderful music, she finds the liberal use of incense, traditional in her church, a bit too overpowering and predictably times her entrance after the processional has passed!

Miriam

# Window #121
# Saint Mark

**Studio Unknown**
**After 1950**

*John Gardner*
*Sept. 2, 1855 – Feb. 22, 1935*

The small clerestory window in the north transept, the third of the four windows in St. Paul's honoring the Gospels, features Saint Mark, the Evangelist. He is depicted as a bearded man wearing a loose fitting white garment with a red cloak and holding a blue book ornamented with a golden budded cross. He has long brown hair, brown eyes, and his skin appears to have been exposed to the sun. His facial expression seems sad or introspective. The banderole over his head reads:

*Take Mark*
*And Bring Him With Thee*
*II Tim IV.11*

**THE STORY:** It is believed that Mark became a follower of Jesus before He died. When Paul was taken prisoner in Rome, he specifically asked Timothy to "take Mark and bring him with you, for he is useful to me for ministering," the words from *Timothy* used in the window. In writing what is proclaimed to be Peter's account of Jesus' work, Mark is thought to have written the plainest, most direct, and most human of the Gospels. Rather than dwell on the past, his gospel records events, describes the feelings of people, the anguish of suffering, and the relief felt by Jesus' touch.

**MEMORIAL:** John Gardner was born in Key West on September 2, 1855. He married Susan Melana Curry on February 1, 1892 in St. Paul's Church, with The Reverend Gilbert Higgs officiating.

For over 30 years, John Gardner worked with the Ferdinand Hirsch Cigar Company as shipping clerk and trimmer. At the time, the cigar industry in Key West was at its height. With civil war unrest taking place in Cuba, much of the cigar industry there moved across the Straits of Florida to Key West. The weather conditions in Key West were perfect for cigar making, and the island had skilled Cuban cigar makers as well as willing local workers like John Gardner who devoted a lifetime to the industry.

John was an active churchman, serving for over 16 years as Sunday School Superintendent of the (First) Holy Innocents Episcopal Church. He was a lay reader, served on the vestry of (First) Holy Innocents and St. Paul's. When (First) Holy Innocents closed its doors in October 1917, he was responsible for saving the records, taking them to St. Paul's where they serve as an important part of their archives today. John died on February 22, 1935 and was buried from St. Paul's three days later.

Saint Mark

# Window #122

# Ascension, Pentecost, Resurrection

**(Left Panel – *Resurrection* - Detail)**
**Phipps, Ball & Burnham**
**Circa 1920**

*William Curry, Father   Euphemia Curry, Mother*
*Charles, George H., Henry F., Robert O. Curry, Brothers*

**DESCRIPTION:** The large clerestory window in the north transept is made up of three themed panels each featuring a defining moment following the crucifixion of Christ: the *Resurrection* (left panel), the *Pentecost* (central panel) and the *Ascension* (right panel).

In the left panel, *Resurrection*, Christ appears to be barely hovering over a thin cloud.  This detail shows three Roman soldiers whose sole duty was to guard the tomb.  Dressed in full uniform, these men appear to have fallen asleep while on duty.

**MEMORIAL:** William Curry was born on September 11, 1821 on Green Turtle Cay, Bahamas, and came to Key West at an early age.  On his birthday in 1844, he married Euphemia Lowe.  His rise to riches in the maritime industry in Key West was phenomenal, and by the time he died in 1896, he was the richest man in Florida.  While much has been written about this self-educated and self-made man, little has been written about an important gift he gave St. Paul's Episcopal Church.

After the great fire of 1886 destroyed much of Key West, including St. Paul's second church, a new wooden structure arose and a chime of 10 bells, the first in the state of Florida, was planned.  William Curry gave the largest bronze bell, fondly called, "Big Bill," weighing nearly a ton and costing $725.00.  It is marked: "Presented by William Curry  Key West, Fla. 1890."  The chime joyously rang out for the first time on Palm Sunday 1891.  Although not recorded, "Big Bill" possibly tolled the passing of William in 1896.

During the 1909 hurricane, the voices of the chimes protested loudly as the church came tumbling down.  By 1919 they were installed in the present church.  Before their centennial, there was a period of silence because the structure of the Bell Tower was weak and "Big Bill" had a cracked yoke.  On Palm Sunday 1991, the 100th birthday of the bells, chime master Joe Lowe briefly rang them in celebration.  That same year they were repaired by McShane & Co., the same company that cast them.

The chime is still part of the life of the church and community.  It sings out boldly above the noise of the city.  If one listens, the lowest tone is the voice of "Big Bill."

# Resurrection
**(Left Panel Detail)**

# Window #122

# Ascension, Pentecost, Resurrection

(Center Panel – *Pentecost* – Detail #1)
**Phipps, Ball & Burnham**
**Circa 1920**

*In loving Memory of My Father William Curry*
*My Mother Euphemia Curry*
*Charles, George H., Henry F., Robert O. Curry, Brothers*

**DESCRIPTION:** The center panel of the large clerestory window in the north transept celebrates the Pentecost, considered to be the birthday of the Christian Church. The panel features a dove enveloped in a white light, with outstretched wings, just below the Gothic canopy; below it are the thirteen people divided into two groups, representing Mary and the twelve disciples.

In this detail, the Holy Spirit, in the form of a dove, is central. The wings are outstretched and the tail is fanned. The nimbus is Tri-Radiant, symbolizing the Holy Trinity; the dove is enveloped in a flood of light.

**THE STORY:** The Pentecost celebrates the descent of the Holy Spirit upon the Apostles. The disciples and Mary, the mother of Jesus, were all gathered in one place. Suddenly, there came a sound from heaven like the rush of a mighty wind. And there appeared to them tongues of fire resting on them. And they were filled with the Holy Ghost. *(Acts 2:1-4)*

**MEMORIAL:** This detail of the center panel is a memorial to the donor's mother, Euphemia Curry, who was born on Green Turtle Cay, Bahamas on February 18, 1829 settling in Key West at an early age with her parents, Captain John Lowe and Bianca Kemp Lowe. Euphemia married William Curry on his birthday, September 11, 1844 with the Reverend W. C. Maloney officiating. William and Euphemia were the parents of eight children: Charles, Louisa, George H., Henry F., Robert O., Eleanor, Florida, and Milton.

Birse Shephard writes in *Lore of the Wreckers* that the Curry's lived in a square house with a ground floor of stone and two upper floors of wood, Bahama style. The front steps led up to the main entrance on the second floor, and there were ample porches around the lower stories. The house was white, inside and out, except for the dining room where the walls were painted light green. It was a comfortable, spacious house, yet no better than those of their neighbors. Indicative of their great wealth, however, the family table was set daily with the famous Tiffany gold table ware that cost $100,000 in the 1880s.

# Pentecost

(Center Panel Detail #1)

# Window #122

# Ascension, Pentecost, Resurrection

(Center Panel – *Pentecost* – Details #2 and #3)

Phipps, Ball & Burnham

Circa 1920

*In Loving Memory of My Father William Curry*
*My Mother Euphemia Curry*
*Charles, George H., Henry F.*
*Robert O. Curry, Brothers*

**DESCRIPTION:** Details #2 and #3 of the center panel of the large clerestory window in the north transept, feature the thirteen people below the dove. In the lower group, (Detail #2) are seven figures of which two are easily identifiable: Saint Mary is dressed in traditional blue and Saint John, often pictured as a youthful, clean shaven man. The remaining five are bearded individuals and represent five of the twelve disciples. Each has a nimbus and a tongue of fires resting on his head: "And there appeared to them tongues as of fire resting on them." *(Acts 2:3)*

In Detail # 3 there are six bearded men of various ages, each with a nimbus with a flame or tongue of fire. They represent the remaining of the twelve disciples. One holds book with a beautifully ornamented cover.

**MEMORIAL:** Of the eight children of William and Euphemia Curry, four are remembered in this window.: Charles was born on June 4, 1847. He married Sarah Jane Lowe on October 8, 1873, with the Reverend John Reuter officiating. He died on May 5, 1898. George Henry was born on December 23, 1851. He married Caroline Albury on April 28, 1873, with the Reverend John Reuter officiating. He died on January 16, 1906. Henry Franklin was born on February 17, 1854, married Susan Fletcher Pinder on February 28, 1880 and lived in Bradenton, Florida. Robert Oliver was born on May 2, 1854, and married Mercedes Valdez on February 11, 1885, with the Reverend F.D. Lune officiating. He died on April 21, 1909.

The four other children of William and Euphemia Curry were Hilton H., Eleanor (Hellings), Florida (Harris) and Louisa (Ann) Porter.

# Pentecost

### (Center Panel Detail #2)

# Pentecost

### (Center Panel Detail #3

# Ascension, Pentecost, Resurrection

(Right Panel – *Ascension* – Detail)
Phipps, Ball & Burnham
Circa 1920

*In loving Memory of My Father William Curry*
*My Mother Euphemia Curry*
*Charles, George H., Henry F., Robert O. Curry, Brothers*

**DESCRIPTION:** The right panel of the north transept clerestory window depicts Christ's Ascension into Heaven.  This detail focuses on the face of a serene Christ.  The artist has pictured Him with brown eyes, hair and beard.  The clothing falls in graceful lines; the nimbus has a cross pattée, and in this detail, only a portion of the light with red rays enveloping Him is seen.  In the full panel Christ is surrounded by a golden aureole, with red rays coming from the aureole.

**MEMORIAL STORY:**  One of the four Curry brothers  remembered here was also remembered with a memorial bell given to (First) Holy Innocents, a mission of St. Paul's (1900-1917), organized by The Reverend Gilbert Higgs, rector of St. Paul's.  The bell was duly marked, but when the author made a special trip to note the memorial marking, she lacked a ladder and a bit of sandpaper and was unable to read the lettering to confirm which of the four brothers' name was on the bell.

At the beginning of the 20th century, bells played an important part in the life of the community and this one was no exception.  They were so important that Father Kelliffer, priest in charge of (First) Holy Innocents, writes that the bell was out of commission for a few days and he was determined to remedy that in short order.

Harold Bethel, a youngster who lived nearby, rang the bell for services for a number of years.  He had a contest with a boy of another church to see who could out-ring the other and lost the wager.  At another time, the bell commenced to ring one evening and, after an investigation, it was found that the rope was tied to the hind end of a cow!

*Ascension*

**(Right Panel Detail)**

# Window #123
# Saint Matthew

**Studio Unknown**
**After 1950**

*To The Glory of God in Loving Memory of*
*George W. Reynolds   1876 - 1926*
*Ida M. Reynolds   1876 – 1947*

**DESCRIPTION:** The window representing Saint Matthew joins the windows of Saint Mark, Saint John and Saint Luke, to complete the quartet of Gospels represented in St. Paul's Church. Matthew is depicted as a bearded man wearing a loose fitting white garment with a bluish green cloak.  In his left hand there is a quill; in his right hand a blue book ornamented with a Latin Cross.  This window, so similar in style to *Saint Mark* (Window #121), whose artist is also not known, was possibly made by the same company.  The banderole over Saint Matthew's head reads:

*Jesus Saw a Man Named Matthew*
*Matt. IX. 9*

**THE STORY**: Matthew, known as Levi before he began following Jesus, was a tax collector.  Early in his ministry, Jesus called Levi, who left everything behind and followed Jesus.  As such, Matthew was one of the first of the 12 disciples.  The former tax collector wrote an inspired account of the life of Jesus Christ from birth to post-resurrection. His gospel, placed first in the New Testament, is a bridge from old to new.  Through Matthew we are told of the relationship of Jesus to the Law and Prophesy of the Old Testament.  Matthew quotes from the Old Testament more frequently than any other New Testament writer.  For example, Matthew opens his gospel with Jesus introduced as the son of David, the king of Israel 1000 years before Jesus was born. *(Matthew 1:1)*

**MEMORIAL:**  George W. Reynolds owed his residence in Key West to the fact that his mother was shipwrecked on the reef off Key West on her way to New Orleans and decided to stay.  George was a cigarmaker, lawyer, and Clerk of the Circuit Court from 1893 to 1905.  He was married to Blanche Stanhope Williams in February 1883, who is remembered in *Raising Jairus' Daughter* (Window #19).  After her death, George married Ida.  George died on September 5, 1926.  Ida died in December 1947, and was buried from St. Paul's with The Reverend James MacConnell officiating.

Saint Matthew

# Christ and the Fishermen

**Harry Taylor**
**1977**

*Daniel L. Navarro, Patricia Lynn Bardecki,*
*Radm. Clyde W. Brunson, Barbara Brunson Sullivan*

**DESCRIPTION:** Along with *Christ with the Elders* (Window #110) in the west wall of the south transept, this clerestory window in the west wall of the north transept is the work a local artist, Harry Taylor. Although thematically different, there is an artistic similarity between the two. In this Taylor window, Christ is shown with fishermen who are hauling in a multitude of fish in their nets. The use of the unusual aqua colored glass gives this window a more contemporary and appropriately tropical feel than the other windows in the church and is most pleasing to the eye.

**THE STORY:** The window, with a theme derived from the sea, can be viewed in two ways. On a spiritual level it tells a story of Christ; on a realistic level, it establishes a connection to the congregation of St. Paul, many of whom made, and continue to make, their living from the sea.

As a biblical narrative it can be interpreted as a wonderful illustration of the manner in which Jesus sought out his disciple, Peter, a fisherman, saying: "Follow me, and I will make you fishers of men." (*Matthew 4: 18-20*) Or, as with the companion window, *Christ with the Elders/Road to Emmaus*, it can be viewed as an illustration of one of the appearances of Christ during the 40 days between His Resurrection and Ascension, which served to strengthen the faith of the disciples. In this Taylor window Jesus manifests Himself to seven of His disciples who had been fishing unsuccessfully on the Sea of Tiberias. Standing on the shore, Jesus told them to cast the net on the right side of the boat to catch the fish. And they did, catching 153. (*John 21*)

**MEMORIAL:** The window was dedicated on Sunday morning, May 15, 1977, by The Reverend Eric W. Potter, rector of St. Paul's. The church bulletin for this service was found in a large trash barrel in a hot, steaming attic of the church by the archivist, along with other correspondence that has been used in this documentation of the windows.

Father Potter headed a procession to the Military Chapel for the dedication of the new clerestory window. He led the congregation in the Window Dedication and Commemoration prayers, remembering Daniel L. Navarro, Patricia Lynn Bardecki, RADM Clyde W. Brunson, and Barbara Brunson Sullivan. The dedication concluded with a prayer for the benefactors, Mrs. Dan L. Navarro and Mrs. Clyde W. Brunson:

*Remember them, O Lord, for good, and grant that all who shall enjoy the benefit of this pious work may show forth their thankfulness to thee by making a right use of the same through Jesus Christ our Lord. Amen*

Christ and the Fishermen

# Window #125

# Holy Trinity or Te Deum

**Phipps, Ball & Burnham (Conjecture)**
**Circa 1920**

**Center Panel:**
*In Loving Memory of*
*Joseph Beverly Browne   1814 - 1888 &*
*Mary Nieves Browne   1824 - 1911*
*Devoted Father and Mother*

**Left Panel:**
*In Loving Memory of*
*Oct. 26, 1845   Livingston W. Bethel   Oct. 21, 1914*

**Right Panel:**
*Robert Jasper Perry   1837 - 1907*
*Elizabeth Browne Perry   1841 - 1891*

**DESCRIPTION:** The large clerestory window on the north side of the nave at the intersection of the transept is comprised of three panels devoted to the Trinity. The focal point, the center panel, is devoted to Christ and representations of the Trinity. Joyous angels on the side panels surround the central theme.

**MEMORIAL:** The entire window was given in memory of various members of the family of Joseph and Mary Nieves Brown. The donors chose to remember the family members as individuals, by dedicating each panel to different ones. As such, each individual family story is told, along with the description of the details of each panel on the pages that follow.

Holy Trinity or Te Deum

# Window #125
# Holy Trinity or Te Deum

(Center Panel Detail #1 and #2)
**Phipps, Ball & Burnham (Conjecture)**
**Circa 1920**

*In Loving Memory of*
*Joseph Beverly Browne   1814 – 1888 &*
*Mary Nieves Browne   1824 – 1911*
*Devoted Father and Mother*

**DESCRIPTION:** The central panel of this glorious window is devoted to the Trinity. God the Father is represented by a hand holding a triangle. His son, Jesus, sits enthroned, with His right hand raised in blessing. His left hand holds a sphere representing the universe. To His right is the symbol of the Holy Ghost, a dove. Kneeling directly below Christ a youthful angel plays the harp. Above the harp are the words: "We Praise Thee Oh God."

**MEMORIAL:** John Eaton Browne and Elizabeth Ann Browne of Windsor, James City County, Virginia, were the parents of twins, Joseph Beverly and Peter Fielding, born on November 6, 1814. At 16 Joseph came to Key West to live. He married Mary Nieves Ximenez, a charming, dark-eyed beauty from St. Augustine, on December 10, 1840. They were the parents of four children.

Joseph had a distinguished career of public service. He was a United States marshal for Florida, Clerk of the U.S. Court, a member of the Legislature of Florida (1866-1870), mayor of Key West several different times, postmaster, and for many years, a warden of St. Paul's.

Mary Nieves of St. Augustine, one of the only other cities of any size in Florida outside of Key West, was the daughter of Mr. and Mrs. Joseph Ximenez. After her marriage to Joseph, she was distinguished for her church and community work. In 1851 she was treasurer of the Ladies Missionary Society of St. Paul's and served as the first president of the Daughters of the King. During the yellow fever epidemics she ministered to the sick. In 1867 she was president of the Confederate Memorial Society. It was sometime during this year that Joseph and Mary Nieves entertained Varina Howell Davis and her husband, Jefferson Davis, president of the Confederacy from 1862-1865.

After Joseph died on December 27, 1888, Mary placed a memorial marble tablet in the third church of St. Paul's. When this wooden church was destroyed in the 1909 hurricane, the memorial tablet, along with others, was saved and was set in the north wall of the present church where it can be seen today.

**Detail #1**

𝕳𝖔𝖑𝖞 𝕿𝖗𝖎𝖓𝖎𝖙𝖞 𝖔𝖗 𝕿𝖊 𝕯𝖊𝖚𝖒
(Center Panel Detail #1 and #2)

**Detail #2**

# Holy Trinity or Te Deum

**(Left Panel Detail)**
**Phipps, Ball & Burnham (Conjecture)**

**Circa 1920**

*In Loving Memory of*
*Oct. 26, 1845   Livingston W. Bethel   Oct. 21, 1914*

**DESCRIPTION:** Whereas the center panel of *Holy Trinity* is devoted to the Trinity, the left panel expresses the joyous praise of angels. It features two beautiful angels, one expressively playing a stringed instrument; the other is prepared to offer a hymn of praise. Above their heads is a banderole with the following words: "And with the morn those angel faces smile." These angels of music and praise were well-chosen as a memorial for a dedicated man.

**MEMORIAL:** Livingston Wellesley Bethel was the son of Judge and Mrs. Winer Bethel. He was born in the Bahamas and came to Key West at an early age. He was educated in Geneva, New York and later studied law. He was district attorney, four term mayor of Key West (1877-1880), Royal Arch Mason, and Knight Templar.

Livingston married Mary Nieves Browne, daughter of Joseph and Mary Nieves Browne, remembered in the center panel of *Holy Trinity*. Livingston and Mary Nieves were the parents of Mary Yulee, Grace Livingston, Henry Livingston, Otto, Florida, Sybil and Effie.

Judge Bethel served St. Paul's and its mission, (First) Holy Innocents, in many capacities. In 1891 when he was Secretary of the Vestry of St. Paul's, his detailed writings preserved the history of its chime of bells, the first chime in the state of Florida. At a time when the bells were in need of repair, this valuable information provided a lead to the same company that cast the bells one hundred years before. A medley of hymns chosen from the bells' inaugural program on Palm Sunday 1891 was heard once again on the anniversary of their one hundredth year.

Holy Trinity or Te Deum

(Left Panel Detail)

# Window #125
# Holy Trinity or Te Deum

**(Right Panel Detail
Phipps, Ball & Burnham (conjecture)
Circa 1920**

*Robert Jasper Perry   1837-1907
Elizabeth Browne Perry   1841-1891
Blessed Parents   Noble Lives*

**DESCRIPTION:** The right panel of *Holy Trinity* completes the feeling of exaltation of the Trinity. Two lovely angels with glorious wings and richly colored garments sing joyously. One is unmistakably singing; the other is strumming a stringed instrument. Above their heads is a banderole which reads:

|  |  |  |
|---|---|---|
| Which | I have Loved | Long |
| Since | And Lost | Awhile |

**MEMORIAL:** The panel is in memory of (Ann) Elizabeth Browne Perry, the daughter of Joseph and Mary Nieves Browne and her husband, Dr. Robert Jasper Perry. At the base of this panel are their names, dates of birth, and the words: "Blessed Parents  Noble Lives."

Ann Elizabeth was one of the most highly educated and accomplished women reared in Key West. "Miss Lizzie," as she was affectionately called, was born on October 18, 1841. In 1854 she entered St. Mary's Hall in Burlington, New Jersey, graduating in 1858. She also studied at the Spingler Institute and graduated in 1861. She was accomplished in music, both vocal and instrumental, and was a fluent French scholar. Upon her return to Key West, she taught in a select school for young ladies. She was a devout member of St. Paul's and for many years the leader of the choir.

Dr. Robert Perry, born in Virginia, moved to Tennessee at an early age. After becoming a physician, he came to Florida, practiced medicine in Key West, and operated a drugstore. He was elected mayor and in 1887 also served as Monroe County Superintendent of Public Instruction. Under his administration, a public school was opened and named "Russell Hall."

Robert and Lizzie were married in 1868 and were the parents of William Y., Sidney R., and an adopted daughter, Rose Forbes.

Holy Trinity or Te Deum
**(Right Panel Detail)**

# Window #126
# *Entry Into Jerusalem*

**(Center Panel Detail)**
**Studio Unknown**
**After 1927   Before 1950**

*Glory to God and In Loving Memory of*
*Thomas Alva Lumley   1861 – 1927*

**DESCRIPTION:**  The entire window is devoted to the triumphal entry of Jesus into Jerusalem one week before His Crucifixion, an event that is celebrated by Christians everywhere as Palm Sunday.  In the center panel, Jesus is seated upon a patient donkey.  His right hand is raised in blessing; his left holds the reins.  A young person stands nearby and looks upon His face with silent contemplation.

**THE STORY:**  On the Sunday before His Crucifixion, Jesus entered the city of Jerusalem astride a donkey.  Great multitudes of people waved palm branches, a symbol of victory and rejoicing, as they went out to meet Him.  Thinking that He might be the Messiah, they cried out: "Hosanna: Blessed is the King of Israel that cometh in the name of the Lord." *(John 12:12-13)'*

**MEMORIAL:**  The window is in memory of Thomas Alva Lumley, a wholesale and retailer of meat.  The son of Thomas and Mary Albury Lumley, remembered in *INRI, Cock, and Sword of the Spirit Roundels* (Window #105), he was born in Key West on December 9, 1861.  In 1884 he married Ruth Demeritt, a native of Key West and the daughter of Mr. and Mrs. John Demeritt.  Thomas and Ruth were the parents of six children: Camille, Rose Marguerite, Flora, Lorraine, and Paul.

Thomas became widely known in the wholesale meat and retail industry and was an important player in the commercial network of Key West.  He was the manager of the Key West slaughter house which was known in the city as "The Butcher Pen" on the Atlantic Ocean, where Rest Beach is today.  In his business, he brought cattle from Punta Rassa, on the mainland of Florida near Fort Myers, and shipped thousands of head of live "beef on the hoof" down the Gulf of Mexico to Key West yearly.

The cattle were unloaded in Key West before dawn.  The cowboys herded the cattle, with the sheriff and police helping astride horses, and Thomas following in his buggy.  In this manner they drove the cattle from the landing at the foot of Duval Street, down Whitehead to South, turning on White Street, and ending up at the slaughter house.  Although the sea has reclaimed the site and scarcely a trace of the Butcher Pen is left, the memory of Thomas Alva Lumley lives on.  Many times the oft-heard jingle was quoted to the author:

*"There's Mr. Lumley*
*Sitting on the fence.*
*Trying to make a dollar*
*Out of ninety-nine cents."*

# Entry into Jerusalem
### (Center Panel Detail)

# Window #126
# Entry Into Jerusalem

**(Left Panel Detail)**
**Studio Unknown**
**After 1927   Before 1950**

*To the Glory of God and In Loving Memory of*
*Thomas Alva Lumley    1861 – 1927*

**DESCRIPTION:** The left panel of *Entry Into Jerusalem* features some of the multitudes gathered to watch Jesus' entry into Jerusalem.  Of the four adults in this panel, three are bearded men; the fourth is a woman.  Although the woman's face is not shown, she has luxurious raven hair held in place with a comb.  Her garments of lovely colors are draped beautifully and she is adorned with golden earrings and a bracelet.  Although one of the men holds a palm frond above his head, his facial expression, and that of the other men, shows no joy.

**MEMORIAL:** Thomas Lumley was considered a fortunate man of his times.   Although he was reputed to be frugal, he was generous to his family, providing a business for his son, Paul, and homes of their own for his daughters.

He had a buggy pulled by a horse that knew the way home under all circumstances.  He was considered a fair man in his business practices and he is remembered for his humor and practical jokes.

In addition to his beef cattle operation, he had a retail store.  One day a lady came into his store to purchase an item that he did not have.  She was persistent and came by so often that Thomas decided to do something about her inquiries.  He bought stray cats at five cents apiece and when he had acquired a sufficient number, he put them in a barrel before his frequent customer arrived.  When she asked if the item had arrived yet, he pointed to the barrel.  She removed the cover and out jumped the cats!  Mr. Lumley might have lost a customer, but the joke is still remembered.

## Entry Into Jerusalem
(Left Panel Detail)

# Entry Into Jerusalem

**(Right Panel Detail)**
**Studio Unknown**
**After 1927   Before 1950**

*To the Glory of God and Loving Memory*
*Thomas Alva Lumley   1861 – 1927*

**DESCRIPTION:** In the right panel of the narrative window depicting Jesus' entry into Jerusalem there is a group of four adults and three children.  One woman carrying a water jug has paused for a moment to watch.  Two bearded men stare in disbelief, as does a third. Three children lead the procession and are engaged in strewing flowers and palms before His path. In addition to using the palm as a sign of victory, the artist has used open faced flowers to symbolize the innocence of children and the sunflower to represent adoration.  The entire window has a distinct green cast, creating the impression of an abundance of foliage.

**MEMORIAL:**  Life in Key West at the end of the 19th century is well depicted through the stories surrounding Thomas Alva Lumley who is remembered in this magnificent window.  His daughter, Ruth, visited Punta Rassa, the point of departure from the mainland of the Gulf coast of Florida near Fort Myers, many times as a young girl and later in life recalled those days of her youth.  She watched the cowboys round up the cattle and put them in a pen near the landing.  When they were ready to load the 200 or 300 head, the men got on the fences, shouting and shaking large lard cans filled with rocks. The frightened animals charged up the railed gangplank of the ship and into the vessel.

On one trip the weather was so severe that Rose was tied to a chair in the mess hall so that she would not be washed overboard.  It could have been a frightening experience on the tossing boat with men manning the pumps for dear life and cows bumping their heads together making mournful sounds. But Rose said she was young and knew little fear.  However, her anxious father, waiting for the boat to arrive in Key West, was concerned and stationed men in the cupolas to look for the vessel and report to him once it was sighted.

## Entry Into Jerusalem
(Right Panel Detail)

# Window #127
# The Transfiguration

**Charles J. Connick Associates**
**1962**

*Jennie Lucille Seymour*
*In Memoriam*
*Nellie Seymour Morris*

**DESCRIPTION:** The descriptive narrative clerestory window on the north side of the nave is divided into three panels depicting the *Transfiguration of Christ*. Christ is featured in the center panel. Moses, holding a tablet representing the Ten Commandments, and one of Jesus' disciples are in the left panel; the prophet Elijah and two other disciples comprise the right panel.

**THE STORY:** The Transfiguration, a miraculous event said to be the culminating point in the earthly life of Jesus, was witnessed by three of his disciples, Peter, James and John. According to the Gospels, Jesus led these three up a mountain "And was transfigured before them: and his face did shine as the sun, and his raiment was white as the light." (*Matthew 17: 2*) This glorious event strengthened the faith of his disciples, preparing them for what lay ahead: "While he yet spake, behold, a bright cloud overshadowed them: and behold a voice out of the cloud, which said, This is my beloved Son, in whom I am well pleased; hear ye him." (*Matthew 17: 5*) Moses, representing the Law and the prophet Elijah, representing the Prophets, also appeared with Jesus, establishing a continuity from the Old Testament.

**MEMORIAL:** The window is in remembrance of Nellie (Ellen) May Seymour Morris and Jennie Lucille Seymour. The donor was Jennie Seymour herself, who left instructions in her will for its installation following her death.

Nellie and Jennie were the daughters of Hiram and Leonora Seymour, remembered in *Crucifixion* (Window #117). Their father, Hiram, was from the Bahamas, settled in Key West, and operated a grocery store. Nellie (Ellen M.) was born on March 15, 1874; Jennie Lucille on March 26, 1879. Other children were Charles E., Hiram C., John C. and Mary E.

Nellie married George Franklin Morris, a native of Ohio on January 7, 1903, with The Reverend Gilbert Higgs, rector of St. Paul's officiating. George was the owner of the Columbia Steam Laundry, and later became a Ford car dealer with the firm Trevor & Morris.

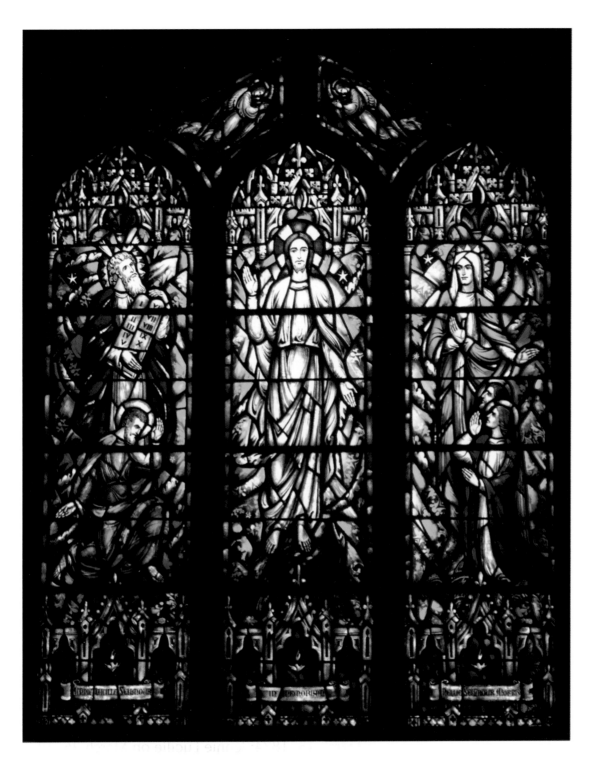

The Transfiguration

# Window #127
# The Transfiguration

(Center Panel Detail)
**Charles J. Connick Associates**
**1962**


*Jennie Lucille Seymour*
*In Memoriam*
*Nellie Seymour Morris*


**DESCRIPTION:** In the center panel detail of The Transfiguration, Christ appears as a barefoot young man wearing loose fitting garments in shades of white, pale yellow and the palest of lavender. These colorations are used effectively to give the illusion of light coming from Christ as it is written that on this occasion Jesus' "face shown as the sun and his outer garments became brilliant with the light." (*Matthew 17:2*) The right hand is raised, the left lowered, with both palms facing outward. Surrounding His head is a Tri-Radiant Nimbus, representing the Trinity.

**THE WINDOW:** This portrayal of the Transfiguration was chosen by The Reverend Edward M. Pennell, Jr., rector of St. Paul's. It is indeed fortunate that the original contract for the window was found in the archives, as it offers a look into the detailed process of selecting a window.

The cost was quoted at $4000. The glass was to be English antique and rolled glass or glass equal in quality. The color of the work and all painting upon the glass was to be a true and fair interpretation of the spirit of the sketch or color design. Other items concerned various specifications. The contract is dated October 30, 1962, and the signatures included those of Orin E. Skinner, president of the studio, and Ruth M. Hunter. This was approved by the rector of St. Paul's and two members of the vestry.

In contrast to the earlier windows of Phipps, Ball & Burnham and Payne Spiers, the figures in the Connick narrative windows, *The Transfiguration* and *Christ Among the Doctors* (Window #108) appear more two-dimensional, somewhat in the manner of Byzantine or Orthodox icons.

# The Transfiguration

**(Center Panel Detail)**

# The Transfiguration

(Left Panel Detail)
**Charles J. Connick Associates**
**1962**

### *Jennie Lucille Seymour*

**DESCRIPTION:** In the left panel of *The Transfiguration*, Moses appears as the topmost figure and is easily recognizable holding the Ten Commandments. Below him is one of the three disciples present at the Transfiguration. It is not possible to discern whether he is Peter, James or John. The other two are featured in the right panel, along with the Prophet Elijah. The placement of Moses and one of the disciples in one side panel and Elijah and the other two disciples in the other establishes a link between the Laws and the Prophecy of Old Testament and the teachings of the New Testament.

**MEMORIAL:** Whereas the entire window devoted to the Transfiguration remembers both Seymour sisters, the donor, Jennie Lucille, is separately noted in the inscription at the base of the left panel.

A delightful person with a ready wit and humor, she had a varied number of interests in life. Jennie was born in Key West, was a Yoemanette during World War I, a time when Key West was home to a Navy base of substantial size, and for many years was teacher in the Monroe County school system.

In later years she lived with her widowed sister-in-law, Emma, on Elizabeth Street. As one entered the house, there was a Victorian coat rack in the hallway. On more than one occasion, Jennie would point to this piece of furniture and draw attention to brother Charlie's summer straw hat and cane hanging there. She would then proceed to tell the visitor that if perchance an intruder would enter the home, they would have a measure of protection because Charlie's hat and cane would indicate that a man lived there. Charlie was long dead and it would be a rare person on the small island who did not know this, but she enjoyed pointing out advantages.

Jennie was a contributor to the leprosy fund for a colony in Louisiana, saving coins in a bank in the shape of a small pig, which, at intervals were sent to the colony. One evening as Jennie and Emma were counting the coins, Amy Shine came to call. Amy contributed the loose change from her purse and was directed by the hostess to go into another room to get the pocketbooks on the bed to fatten the pig. Upon entering the room, Amy encountered a robber who grabbed the pocketbooks and exited through the window.

Although Charlie's hat and cane failed to do the job, Jennie knew what to do. She found her police whistle, kept just in the event of such an occasion, rushed out of the house and blew its shrill tones, but to no avail. The night visitor had fled, leaving behind his shoes, neatly placed under the window!

# The Transfiguration
### (Left Panel Detail)

# Cross and Key Roundel, Saint Andrew Roundel, Pillar and Scourge Medallion

**Phipps, Ball & Burnham**
**1920**
**10' 2 1/2 " x 7'10"**

*Margaret M. Mora   1849 – 1891*
*Fred Howard Matthews   1888 – 1917*

**DESCRIPTION:** Windows #128, #129, and #130 in the north tower are listed as three windows, but are considered one. As is the companion window in the south tower, it is one window comprised of three panels, each featuring a roundel or medallion depicting a Sign of Our Faith. Starting from the right is the *Cross and Key*; in the center is the *St. Andrew Roundel*, a cross in the form of an X; on the left is the *Pillar and Scourge*.

**SYMBOLISM:** The *Cross and Keys Roundel* is a symbol of the apostle Peter who met his death by crucifixion. The crossed keys refer to the Lord's gift to him: the keys of the Kingdom of Heaven.

The *Cross Saltire/St. Andrew Roundel* is a symbol of Saint Andrew, who was put to death in Greece by crucifixion on a cross in the shape of an X. Tradition says that the apostle Andrew died on this form of cross, requesting that he be crucified on a cross unlike that of his Lord.

The Pillar and Scourge symbolizes the Passion. Christ was scourged, or whipped, after His trial before He was lead to Calvary.

**MEMORIAL:** Margaret M. Mora was born in Florida in 1849. Her mother was born in New York; her father in Virginia. She was first married to Antonio Matthews, a baker born in Portugal or the Canary Islands. They were the parents of Harriet, Maria, Edward, and Charles. After the death of Antonio, she married Jose Augustin Mora on August 30, 1875. The Reverend Fulwood, pastor of the First Methodist Episcopal Church, performed the ceremony. The Mora family lived on Eaton Street, near Thomas Street.

Fred Matthews, son of Margaret's daughter, Harriet, was born in Key West in 1888. In 1909 he married Marjorie Fae Fulford. The rector of St. Paul's, The Reverend Charles Stout, performed the ceremony. The year before, Fred founded the daily newspaper *The Journal*, of which he was editor and publisher.

Cross and Key Roundel, Saint Andrew Roundel,
Pillar and Scourge Medallion

# The Windows of the Choir Room & Sacristy

Through the doors on either side of the chancel and out of sight of the congregation are the sacristy and the choir room, two rooms where those who give of themselves so selflessly to St. Paul's Church gather to work. A total of six windows grace these rooms, all recent additions to the stained glass art of St. Paul's by Powell Brothers & Sons, adding glorious light to those few who work on behalf of so many.

## Sacristy Windows:

It is in the sacristy, softly permeated with the scent of incense, that the Altar Guild and Flower Guild prepare the church for services. They do so in the light of two Powell Studio windows honoring their work.

Flower Guild

*The Flower Guild* is represented by a simple flower stalk bearing three white Easter lilies on the signature Powell ground of intensely colored glass rectangles. These lilies serve the dual purpose of representing the work of the Flower Guild and symbolizing immortality and the Resurrection and, as there are three, the Trinity.

*Altar Guild* honors the work of the Altar Guild through an artistic representation the vessels holding the Elements: the sacramental wine and bread used in Holy Communion.

Altar Guild

# Choir Room Windows

The Choir Room, behind a door on the right side of the chancel, could be called Joe Lowe's room as it has been the domain of St. Paul's masterful organist and choir director since 1970. In this room where the choir gathers, are four Powell windows: two depicting angels; a third, Saint Cecelia; a fourth, a young King David. All are appropriately playing musical instruments and are artistically rendered in the Powell style: solitary figures set against a background of rectangular panes of vividly colored glass.

*Angel with Lute*

Surrounded by these recent additions, Joe Lowe marvels at the added dimension they give the choir room. At certain times of day, when the light is just right, the room comes alive, not just with color, but with shimmering patterns of light reflected on the walls by the distinctive ripples in the glass.

*Angel with a Lute*, depicting an angel in a simple robe in shades of green and brown playing a lute, remembers Margaret Monsalvatge. In the words of Choir Director Lowe, "Margaret was a choir member and one of the dearest members of the Church." It is a testament to her that so that many parishioners, as well as her generous family, participated in the purchase of the window. In her later years, as she was losing her sight, parishioners picked her up every Sunday to bring her to church.

*Angels with Flutes* featuring two angels in garments in shades of brown playing the flute, was given by Jenkyn Powell of Powell Brothers & Sons Glass Art in memory of his wife, Valorie Clare Hatsis Powel. Although not a member of St. Paul's, Jenkyn Powell chose to honor those dearest to him in a church far from his Utah home.

*Angels with Flutes*

*David Playing the Lyre* features David, the son of Jesse (*Jesse Tree - Window #102*) and ancestor of Jesus, who wisely governed the tribes of Israel. As a youth known for skillfully playing the lyre, he was called upon by King Saul to ease his troubled mind. (*1 Samuel 16: 14-23*) In a double entendre, blended into the art strokes of the lyre is a church mouse, for the ever-present Joe Lowe, honoree, and Luther's rose, a tribute to the Lutheran heritage of the donors, David D. and Irene Eyre.

The window honors and recognizes the dedication and contribution to St. Paul's of the man who has carried out his life's work in this room: Joe Lowe, Organist and Choir Director. The choice of the story of the young David, the noted musician, as the subject for the window is an appropriate tribute to Joe, whose wonderful and inspirational music has filled St. Paul's for so many years. The donors, David and Irene Eyre, involved parishioners

David playing the Lyre

of St. Paul's who now call Key West home after vacationing on the island for many years, wanted to honor Joe for his enormous contributions to St. Paul's.

The fourth window in the choir room, *Saint Cecelia*, is yet another generous donation from Jenkyn Powell of Powell Brothers & Sons Glass Art, this one in memory of his mother, Doris Auleen Napper Powell. Most suitable for the choir room, it features the patron saint of music, Saint Cecelia, playing the organ.

Saint Cecelia

# Epilogue

As one of the most recent windows to be dedicated in St. Paul's, *David Playing the Lyre* reflects on-going work of the church and captures the spirit of *The Golden Cockerel*.

The pictorial reference to David and his gift of music provides a biblical story beautifully rendered through the glorious artistry of painted light.

Organist and choir director Joe Lowe, the individual it honors, has filled St. Paul's with music for 35 years. He has given his gift to the congregation for so long that his glorious music is as much a part of the essence of the church as are the beautiful windows. Joe also represents the generational conti-nuity of families who have established the deep and solid roots so evident in the island community. Born in Key West, Joe is a seventh generation Conch, a descendent of the brother of John Lowe, Jr., donor of the center panel of the *Crucifixion* (Window #117), whose family originally came from the Bahamas.

Since its first settlers, people moving to Key West have brought with them ideas and customs from their place of origin, contributing to its unique character. Whereas many of the early settlers came here through the maritime, cigar and fishing industries, most present day residents come from a myriad of backgrounds and professions and are lured to the island after a first encounter as a tourist.

If Joe is a link to the past, the donors of the window, David and Irene Eyer, who first came to Key West on vacation, represent the present. Exemplifying the on-going generosity and involvement of the con-gregation of St. Paul's in their church and in their community, they add yet another important layer to the permanent foundation of this interesting island

In St. Paul's Church, the Eyers have found a community within a community. According to David, in this special church on this unique island he has found something beyond the gratification of attend-ing inspirational services in a beautiful church filled with magnificent windows. Amid "a wonderful mixed up bunch of people, both those whose families have been here for generations and relatively new ones like me, I have found that 95 percent of what you receive from the experience is in your heart and mind. The parishioners make it that way."